GENERAL GEORGE S. PATTON ON
ACCELERATING PERFORMANCE
IN TODAY'S BUSINESS WORLD

GET

TO

KNOW

ME

GENERAL GEORGE S. PATTON ON
ACCELERATING PERFORMANCE
IN TODAY'S BUSINESS WORLD

Chuck Gumbert

PUBLISHING

For information on distribution rights, royalties, derivative works or licensing opportunities on behalf of this content or work, please contact the publisher at the address below or via email info@nolimitpublishinggroup.com.

COMPANIES, ORGANIZATIONS, INSTITUTIONS, AND INDUSTRY PUBLICATIONS: Quantity discounts are available on bulk purchases of this book for reselling, educational purposes, subscription incentives, gifts, sponsorship, or fundraising. Special books or book excerpts can also be created to fit specific needs such as private labeling with your logo on the cover and a message from a VIP printed inside.

No Limit Publishing Group
123 E Baseline Road, D-108
Tempe AZ 85283
info@nolimitpublishinggroup.com

This book was printed in the United States of America

No Limit Publishing
No Limit Enterprises, LLC
1601 E 69th Street, Suite 200
Sioux Falls, SD 57108

DEDICATION

This book could not have been written had it not been for the loving support given to me by my parents and family.

And in memory of my father, Charles E. Gumbert, who while growing up, provided me the guidance, encouragement, and foundation that have allowed me to take advantage of the numerous opportunities that have come my way.

Without him as a role model, mentor, and supporter, I would not be in the position I am in today. Thanks Dad.

A CODE OF ACTION

George S. Patton, 1917

I didn't begin with the askings
I took my job and stuck
I took the chances they wouldn't
And now they are calling it luck.

In wondrous catlike ability
For grasping all things which go by
To land on my feet with agility
No one is greater than I.

In doing the things others will not
In standing the blows others shirk
In grasping the chance that returns not
And never yet shirking my work.

CONTENTS

INTRODUCTION

"The great things a man does appear to be great only after they are done. When they are at hand, they are only normal decisions and are done without knowledge of their greatness."

"The results prove that, as ever, leadership and audacity bring success."

General George S. Patton

Like every other boy growing up in the 1950s and 60s, I had uncles and neighbors who fought in WWII and Korea. I saw the movies: *The Battle of Britain, The Longest Day, Patton, Thirty Seconds Over Tokyo, The Great Escape*, and all of the other war movies of the time. I watched the WWII TV series: "Combat," "Twelve O'Clock High," "Rat Patrol," and others. After school and on weekends the neighborhood kids and I played "Army" with our toy guns, uniforms, and helmets. Growing up in that environment had a major impact on my life. I was amazed at the commitment and massive undertaking it took to make the events of WWII successful. And leaders, especially the military leaders, made a great impression on me even at that early age.

In the 1950s and 60s Americans had great pride in our country and ourselves. Patriotism ran high and we rallied around the American flag and all it represented. The Pledge of Allegiance was recited in schools without controversy (with the word God) and the "Star Spangled Banner" was proudly sung at all civic and sporting events. It was not like today when it's a hit-or-miss activity and during which you routinely see men wearing hats, people talking, eating, chatting on their cell phones or just sitting there. I find this behavior to be disrespectful to our nation and to those who fought to keep it free. The flag, Pledge of Allegiance, and "Star Spangled Banner" were significant parts of the belief system we had in our country and our vision for ourselves and the future. Our focus was on family, education, and technology, and these values were communicated and supported by our elected and respected government officials and business leaders. We were proud of our country and we wanted to continue to see it grow, flourish, and prosper. Back then, we knew where we were going. We had a vision, we had a plan, and that kept us together and helped us move forward as a nation.

The impression made upon me during my childhood carried over into my adult life. In the early 1990s, while getting ready for an overseas business trip, I was looking for a book to read. Walking through an airport bookstore, I picked up the book *War as I Knew It*, by General George S. Patton. This book, published after his death in 1945, was an autobiographical account of Patton's actions during WWII. As I read the book I became intrigued with the man, who he was, what he thought, and how he thought. I also noted how his success was connected with his straightforward, no-nonsense approach in everything from leadership to strategy, planning, discipline, operations, and training. Over the next couple of years I read several other books about General Patton and saw many similarities between running a business and a military operation or an army.

Today, as I watch the news, there are two things I particularly notice in the events unfolding that concern me: the lack of leadership and the lack of a clearly defined direction (a vision and strategy) about where we are going and how we are going to get there successfully. This is true not only for the nation, but for its many businesses as well.

There are a lot of important issues facing the United States right now, but as a nation, it's not really clear where we are headed. We have ideas and concepts about what needs to be addressed, but it seems that no one knows how to do so, or is willing to take a firm stand and lead us in addressing them. What is the plan? What are we going to do? We've lost our identity and this lost identity and the current underlying philosophy that we must keep everyone happy as we strive to be politically correct, prevent us from creating a clear and definitive plan because we are afraid of stepping on anyone's toes. We're lost in a sea of ambiguity.

General Patton was very big on planning, and his philosophy was to "Go Forward. Always Go Forward!" To "Go Forward," however, we need a clear objective and a plan for *how* to meet that objective. His quote, "A good plan violently executed today, is better than the perfect plan next week," fits well with where we currently are as a country. But what's the objective? What's the plan? Where are we going?

Over the past 20 years, there has been a lot of talk about the "Republicans this," and the "Democrats that," but no real leadership or common goal or objective to pull us together. As a result, it's not clear where we are going. No direction. No leadership. No plan. The alignment we shared in the 1950s and 60s is no longer evident, because today we lack a vision and plan that we all know, see, understand and believe in as a nation. Many of us remember the inspiring words of President Kennedy's inaugural address, "Ask not what your country can do for you, but what you can do for your country." Now we look at it from the other side and are centered on what the country can do (or give) to us. We've shifted our beliefs 180 degrees and to me that's backwards! We have lost our strong sense of patriotism, our common goals and objectives, and as a result, we have lost our identity, direction, and strength as a nation. From my perspective, this is just wrong!

As an example, during the writing of this book the national unemployment rate was a major issue and discussion point in the mainstream media. One month it was up, but then the next month it was down, and all the talking heads and elected officials in Washington, D.C. told us nothing of the plan to improve the situation. We heard the numbers, but no news as to what was being done to remedy the issue and get people back on the job. Nor did they discuss what constitutes the real rate of employment (or unemployment). For example, the news never mentioned the unemployed folks who have been looking for work so long that their unemployment benefits had run out and were no longer included in the unemployment calculation, people who had stopped looking for work, or the people who had taken lower level positions at a lesser salary just to stay afloat. The unemployment figures were just numbers and grossly understated numbers, and there was no real plan to improve the unemployment situation in this country. It was just talk. There was no real plan. We were depending upon hope, and where I come from, hope is not a strategy. To me, and I think Patton would feel the same way, reporting numbers is a whole lot different than having a real plan.

Another area where we seem to be blindly forging ahead is our world affairs. Again, where is America's plan regarding world affairs? I just don't see it today. I see us out in the world apologizing for what some people feel are the wrongs this country has committed in the past, and we allow these apologies to continue. There are politicians and people who seem to forget history and where we would be as a nation had the U.S. not taken a stand and bold action. What do we stand for today, and who are we as a nation? It seems that in today's America we fall short of taking a definitive stand on any issue for fear that we may upset someone. Instead we bow down to try to please everyone and then wonder why we aren't making any progress or end up being taken advantage of. We no longer have a clearly defined vision for America and as a result, we don't know who we are or where we are going. We've lost our identity, our direction, and to a certain extent, our pride.

Patton ran into a very similar situation in March 1943 when he took over the U.S. Army's II Corps after their poor performance against the Germans at Kasserine Pass in North Africa. When he took over the ragtag unit, there was little or no leadership, lack of discipline, and the direction was unclear. There was limited accountability and minimal understanding of the plan. In very short order, after taking command, Patton established a back to basics approach with a clear understanding of his vision, which highlighted what was important, where they were going, and how they were going to get there. Known for his strong leadership abilities, Patton had a hard charging approach to everything he touched and a high level of energy, drive, and expectations for himself and his troops. He admired and respected his troops and most felt the same for him. He always had a vision and plan for his organization that was well communicated and understood by all. He knew where he was going and provided the leadership the unit needed in order to work together and execute the plan. And his methods proved successful as illustrated by his victory against General Rommel's German troops at El Guettar shortly after taking command. Patton's leadership and simple no nonsense, back to basics approach worked for him during WWII, and if we follow his example, it will work just as well for America and today's business to Move Forward.

After 35 years of business experience I've seen all the fancy, magic, whiz-bang, academic, flavor of the month approaches to running, changing, and operating a business. Although some have their strong points, I have found that many are not sustainable due to the lack of leadership, vision, strategy, commitment, and the follow-through required to make them viable and successful. The concepts and philosophies of General George S. Patton are very similar to my own, and I've been able to incorporate them successfully into the day-to-day aspects of business operational turnarounds, and the enhanced performance of the normal, daily operations.

Like Patton, I have always been a firm believer in the need for having a vision, strategy, or plan and strong leadership to execute that plan. I think to get America and today's business world Moving Forward we need to incorporate more of the straightforward and back to basics approach demonstrated by Patton. It worked for him and it's worked for me. By approaching our businesses in the same manner, we can *Move Forward* and *Accelerate the Performance* of our organizations and our nation. If we follow General Patton's lead, we can once again rise to greatness as a nation.

CHAPTER 1
MEET THE AUTHOR

"If everyone is thinking alike, then somebody isn't thinking."

"Go Forward!!! Always Go Forward!!!"

General George S. Patton

I've been asked on several occasions why I am writing this book. The purpose is to share my knowledge, expertise, and experiences with others. I've seen too many businesses that focus far too much on the financials and lose sight of Vision-Mission-Purpose. This is true whether it's coming from the board of directors, the owner, the president, or the general manager. This happens automatically as you push the organization to deliver without showing them *how* to plan and deliver. My business, **The Tomcat Group** was established to help organizations learn *how* to develop and deliver on that plan. In this chapter I have included several personal examples to illustrate how I have come to learn that Patton's system of leadership is the most effective and complete, and will spend the rest of the book sharing with you how you can implement these strategies into your own enterprise effectively.

As I mentioned earlier, I grew up in the 1960s, and at an early age became intrigued with the events of WWII and the military in general. In listening to the stories of my uncles and neighbors, I found myself fascinated by the leaders of that time. They were heroes to me. I looked up to them and found myself drawn to them and their experiences. Military leadership made an impression upon me as I realized that these men's decisions made a difference, an impact, on thousands, maybe millions of lives, and on history.

When I was 18 years old I began working for a company that refurbished jet engine components for airline and military customers. It was a dirty job and the summer temperatures inside the north Texas facility were well in excess of 110 degrees. I hated that job, but little did I know how influential it would be. It was there that I met a 40-year-old man who indirectly helped me put my life in order. This man was married with three children and was getting paid only a little more than I was. In talking to him I heard a lot of, "I wish that I had gone to college," "I wish I had joined the military," and "I wish I hadn't gotten married so young." The man wasn't necessarily unhappy, but it seemed he had a lot of regrets about what might have been if he had just done a few things differently. He didn't have a plan for his life. His life was a series of random events. At that point I made the decision that I was not going to be one of those people who looked back on his life and said, "I wish I had…" The decision was to do things differently so I wouldn't be the one expressing my regret to an 18-year-old kid twenty years later.

It was that first summer out of high school when I put my life plan together. As part of that plan, I began flying lessons and obtained my private pilot license, which was part of a greater plan to fly military jet fighters. Over the next five years, I continued to work at that repair shop while attending college, including full time during the summer break. In December 1977, after obtaining my Bachelors of Business Administration degree from the University of Texas at Arlington, I reported for duty at the U.S. Navy Aviation Officer Candidate School (AOCS) in Pensacola, Florida. There I became a Naval Officer and in 1984 finished my career flying the F-14 *Tomcat* fighter aircraft. During my time in the Navy I held several junior officer positions and was led by some captivating, motivating, and outstanding leaders. It was also during that time that I learned a lot about myself and about life.

It was while in the military and flying high performance aircraft that I learned the critical aspects of discipline and attention to detail. Bringing an F-14 *Tomcat* aboard a carrier is not something done casually, especially if you have lost your hydraulics, are landing at night, flying in bad weather, or confronted with a pitching carrier flight deck. These are the times when you must have confidence in yourself and your flying abilities, but also the capability to maintain coolness under pressure. This is where the training and discipline pay off. In these situations you learn to listen, follow instructions, and execute procedures while maintaining the focus to recognize subtle changes in the details and a full understanding of the big picture, or what we called "situational awareness." It's not easy. Later, I recognized that these attributes, which were so critical to me at the time, would also be key elements in operating a successful business.

My military experience reinforced my belief in the need to have a plan. Although I had created goals, and worked hard toward fulfilling those goals, I began to understand that to achieve these goals I needed a definitive step by step plan for how each would be achieved, and to visualize what the end result should look like so I could *Go Forward* to the next step. For example, you don't just walk into the U.S. Navy and have the keys to an F-14 handed to you. There was a very well thought out and detailed plan that needed to be followed and executed with specific training qualifications that I needed to meet before getting those keys. And believe me, I wanted those keys!

Whether your goal is to fly a high performance aircraft such as the F-14 or to become the CEO of your own company, it all begins with a vision, which in my case was getting to fly military jet fighters and earning my Navy "Wings of Gold." That was the goal and the plan (or in this case, the curriculum and requirements according to the folks at Naval Air Training Command). The proven training basics, foundation, and regimen were already in place. All I needed to do was progress through that training syllabus from simple maneuvers like taking off and landing, through ever increasing levels of knowledge and difficulty, such as navigation, instrument flying, aerobatics, day and night formation flying, dropping ordnance, air-to-air combat tactics, and flying higher performance aircraft. This eventually culminated with a trip to an aircraft carrier ("The Boat") for my first carrier landings or "traps." I had to fully and successfully complete each step of that training plan (or process) before I received those Wings and the keys to the *Tomcat*.

What I learned during this process was that anyone who wants to achieve something needs a vision (an objective) and a plan to get there. They then need to complete all of the steps that are built into that plan and have the discipline and commitment to follow through and execute. There are (and were) NO SHORTCUTS!

It was while flying that I got another perspective on the need for planning. When getting ready for a flight it was essential to plan the fuel load, weight and balance, ordnance, route, weather, radio frequencies, tanker location, and where the ship was going to be when you got back and your approach speed.

Nothing was left to chance. You planned everything, and in some cases, you had a backup plan, and those planning requirements made quite an impression upon me. Never could I hop into an airplane and just take off. To be successful, there needed to be a plan and the discipline to follow and execute that plan every time. Anything less could have been disastrous. The same is true in running a business. Where are we going and what's the plan?

This was also where I got to experience firsthand the leadership, teamwork, and support necessary for an organization to be successful. Our time at sea wasn't just about how we operated within the squadron, but how each element of the Air Wing and Task Force worked together. We were all there supporting the operation and everyone was aligned in our goals, objectives, and actions. We were all part of the strategy.

After my tenure as a Naval Officer and pilot, I opted to rejoin the civilian world and got my first business role as a customer service manager for a company that overhauled and repaired jet engines. This is where I first discovered that organizational "alignment" is not always a given and as a result conflict could (and would) easily manifest itself. At this company, the operations team was graded and rewarded by the number of engines it shipped, and the sales team was graded and rewarded by the number of engines it brought in. Nowhere was it clear what team was responsible for the cost or how much money the company made as a result of those overhauls, and this resulted in problems. The month-end discussions and finger pointing centered on whether or not the engine was quoted properly or if operations handled it properly during the repair process. I often wondered why we weren't working together. Why was this allowed to happen? Was I the only one who saw that things were misaligned and that if both departments had the same goals and objectives and were graded the same way that we'd be much more profitable? It was common sense to me.

This company was also big on taking care of customers, and it was there that I learned the value of good customer service and the benefits it yields. Because of my dedication to the care of customers, I was hired by one of those customers to help build their business.

Over the next ten years my career focused on business development activities that included winning new business from new and current customers and identifying and developing new products to bring to market. What I learned was that to be able to win business, a salesman needed to sell not only externally to the customer, but internally as well. I've always maintained that while in business development I spent about 75% of my time selling internally. This internal selling was centered on highlighting, preaching, and leading the way as to why we needed to take care of the customer in order to first gain the customer's business and then keep it. I sold the need to deliver customer orders on time and to ensure that the quality of our product and customer service were top notch. However, because the leaders of the organization did not have a clear vision or plan, and were just pushing for shipments or sales, it was difficult to foster this philosophy and lead the way regarding customer care, especially when the primary internal objective was shipments for the sake of dollars.

This was my first experience working in an environment with no direction, constantly changing priorities, and overall chaos. It was also during this time that I had my first experiences working with an underperforming business that lacked a plan. This situation was both frustrating and painful, and I was determined to find a better way.

The corporate board of directors had given the organization a directive to attain a set financial target for the year, but provided no guidance as to how to get there. The resulting day-to-day activities were extremely chaotic with everyone under pressure to "make the month." To make matters worse, the general manager was struggling to pull it together. I realized that this insanity stemmed from the lack of a clear vision or strategy on which the organization could focus.

This business was actually two business units in one. They had one segment that manufactured new products and another that provided aftermarket or overhaul services to a different set of customers. With the two market segments, products, and customers, the organization struggled with two opposing and sometimes competing mindsets, philosophies, and priorities of new manufacture versus overhaul. Operating together, each of these business segments impeded the organization's ability to *Move Forward* as it struggled to meet customer demands and financial directives in an environment of ever changing priorities.

There was no overall plan and the focus was strictly to make the numbers. I recognized this as something that kept the company from getting to where it needed to go to truly realize success. Contemplating a potential solution, I realized the need and benefit of operating these two diverse business segments as separate entities. After all, in every aspect they were fundamentally different and each was holding the other back. I prepared and submitted a plan to the general manager to split the business into two segments, to provide separate and dedicated leadership and operational teams for each entity so as to put the appropriate focus on both business units. He openly and flatly rejected the plan, calling it idiotic, and questioned my business common sense. Convinced that splitting the business and putting a distinct and focused plan together for each segment was the right thing to do, like Patton I took a bold, audacious, and potentially career ending move. I sent the plan to the president. He read it, saw the merit in making the split, and after some good spirited discussions, approved the plan.

At that point I was given the opportunity to run the aftermarket business unit with profit and loss responsibility. From there we prepared separate strategic, sales, operations and financial plans for each business unit and incentive plans that were structured for each business. The results were impressive. The aftermarket grew by 65% within the first year and 18 months later moved to a larger facility to handle the growth. The manufacturing side also grew dramatically and we built a new facility the following year to handle its growth. Overall, by splitting the business into separate and distinct business units, and developing a plan for each, we were able to eliminate the daily conflicts and chaos and successfully grow the business by 200% over the next three years. As a result of these accomplishments, the general manager was promoted to president responsible for several business units and I was promoted to plant manager, overseeing both the aftermarket and manufacturing sides of our business.

This experience taught me that by having faith in my abilities and the courage to stand up in the face of adversity and offer a unique and different approach and plan contrary to the current management philosophy, and the passion to stick to those convictions, I could make a positive and lasting change. Almost 20 years later, that business still operates successfully as two separate entities.

The next opportunity I was offered was to lead my own operational turnaround as the VP and General Manager for an organization that provided jet engine component aftermarket services for a larger division that overhauled the engines. At the time, the organization operated as a captive or satellite facility, and had virtually no customer base outside the larger parent division. The organization had recently been acquired and the new owners found a host of internal issues and problems, which included an attempt amongst the workforce to form a union. I was hired to turn the organization around, improve performance, keep the union out, and gain new third party business. This was a challenging opportunity.

We developed a plan to accomplish these objectives, enhanced the leadership team with some new talent, and instructed this team to begin working directly with the workforce to understand and remedy their issues and concerns as well as the operational issues. We soon began gaining the trust of the workforce by consistently highlighting and communicating where we wanted to go. With all the positive changes and communication, the union quickly walked away.

Unfortunately, within about four months of the acquisition, we were hit with a crisis: the larger parent division lost a major airline contract that comprised 33% of our total business. Then, a few months later, the parent division lost another large customer and our organization had to replace yet another 33% of the business. Despite these major setbacks, however, we regained what the company had lost within a year through active, strategic selling to new third party customers and the development of new products and capabilities.

As part of the strategy, during the time we were adding new work and customers, we were also working on our process improvement activities with a focus on improving product processing and turn-around times. We knew shorter product turn-around times were key to our growth. Through the teamwork of the leadership and workforce, we were able to process and turn around orders twice as fast as our competition. These shorter product turn-around times and our product line expansion were major selling points to our new customer base and played a significant role in the organization's eventual sale to a major engine manufacturer.

From there I took on another turnaround challenge as the president of a multi-site organization that supplied new manufacture and aftermarket support services for electromechanical components for the aerospace and military markets. This business had recently been acquired, and the business unit's current leadership was not integrating well with the new owners. There was an underlying philosophy that insinuated, "We are different," and "You don't understand our business." These types of comments and adverse mindset kept things from *Going Forward*. Although the business possessed superior engineering and offered a technologically advanced product, on-time delivery to the customer and customer service attributes were lacking. My directive and charter was to put the organization on track and take it to its next level of performance.

With the support and assistance of the parent organization, we developed a plan with the input of the current leadership team, but there were still internal alignment and accountability issues holding back performance. To foster that alignment we implemented a series of performance metrics followed up with specific plans to drive the underperforming metrics. As part of the strategy we developed a method to get prototypes and new products to market in a much shorter timeframe. It typically took nine months to a year to develop a new product, and the customers were looking for a solution much sooner than that. Most of them wanted something within two to three months. At the time, the engineering development activities were mixed in with the daily production activities. Production needs took priority, not only from an engineering perspective, but also for the use of production resources needed to support the engineering activities. There were daily conflicts that impeded operations and engineering development progress. With these issues in mind, we split the engineering development activities away from the day-to-day operations efforts and established a unique, separate, and dedicated development team with the resources to effectively develop new products within two months. It worked and the concept soon paid off when the organization won a major contract award by fulfilling a customer need (Read: problem) in an expedited manner.

The next challenge was as the VP of Operations with an aerospace start-up company that was trying to implement an aircraft cargo-conversion modification program for the 30+ aircraft owned by a major freight company. This conversion entailed the removal of the passenger seats, the overhead bins, galleys, and lavatories and the installation of a new reinforced floor and the supporting structure of the cargo modification. Upon my arrival, the program was already two years behind schedule. The company had the drawings, the FAA approval, and the facilities, but not the labor or support network needed to complete the job effectively. To compound matters, the company had committed to the customer to deliver the first 10 aircraft within six months—a major objective.

Very quickly the new team noted that the drawings were flawed, the parts network had not been established, and the labor hours estimated to complete each aircraft were off by over 300%. To say the least, we were not off to a good start, and major issues had to be corrected if we were going to succeed and fulfill the expectations.

We developed and implemented a plan to meet the delivery requirement for the first 10 aircraft on time and began hiring the needed technicians, engineers, and quality people right away. While this was happening, work was underway to address the engineering concerns and getting the parts supply flowing. The workflow was established and the shop documentation set up to turn an aircraft around in less than 30 days from start to finish. We established six staggered aircraft production lines and, despite the issues involved, every aircraft was delivered on-time. Most notably, because of the relationship developed with the customer and the high caliber of the work being performed, we were able to negotiate a significant increase in price.

After that, I took another turnaround position for an aerospace company that machined, fabricated, and assembled structural components for aircraft. This too was a recent acquisition and the integration and operational issues had reduced on time customer delivery to less than 25%, inventory was climbing, scrap and rework were high, cash was bleeding, priorities changed constantly, and the entire organizational focus was to "make the month" in terms of sales dollars. The company was literally in a crisis management situation as both customer and suppliers were upset, the workforce frustrated with the chaos, and the management team too inexperienced to seek and develop a remedy on its own. Over the next year that leadership team would be restructured with some being moved to positions that better suited their skills, backgrounds, and capabilities, while others were removed or moved on.

As part of the turnaround, the team focused on specific goals and objectives tied to inventory and scrap reduction and accelerated throughput, which meant reduced lot or batch sizes and several major process improvements. The biggest change was scheduling the workflow on an oldest job first basis and managing it on a "Theory of Constraints" basis. This was a major cultural shift for the organization, and was not well received by many members of the middle management team that had been with the company for any length of time, but was crucial for the company's success if it was going to *Move Forward*.

The needed organizational alignment and feedback were gained through the use of performance metrics. Part of those metrics was a series of Visual Status Boards placed throughout the shop in critical path areas. These status boards, maintained by the supervisor, listed the schedule for the area and posted any issues/problems that were impacting the schedule, such as material shortages, engineering issues, or maintenance needs. These boards proved to be very beneficial communication tools in highlighting daily progress to anyone coming through the area, including senior management. The facility was dirty inside and out, cluttered with old, dilapidated, and unused equipment and junk was everywhere. To top it off, the employee restrooms were atrocious. A major clean up campaign was established, the old junk, the abandoned equipment hauled away, and the restrooms were updated. As a result of our efforts, within nine months, on-time delivery had improved to 75%, scrap had been reduced by 400%, inventory reduced by 30%, and profitability and cash improved dramatically. We weren't there yet, but were well on our way. This was quite an accomplishment given the initial set of circumstances, and by far the largest and most complicated turnaround I have conducted. I give the credit to the leadership team and the entire workforce for their input, participation, and follow through.

Once completing that project in late 2009 I established *The Tomcat Group* with a focus on assisting other organizations in *Accelerating Business Performance* by utilizing the experience, expertise and toolkit I've developed over the years.

In summary, I have over 35 years in business with the last 15 years centered on financial and operational turnarounds. In that time I have participated in or led seven successful turnarounds in the following new manufacture and aftermarket aerospace markets:

1. Turbine Engines
2. Turbine Engine Component Overhaul
3. Aircraft Electromechanical Components
4. Aircraft Structures, Structural Components, and Assemblies
5. Instrument and Avionics

With the downturned economy, there are too many organizations focused only on the moment, which has taken the attention away from planning for the future. By cutting everything to the bare bones and only looking at the short term, they are adversely affecting their tomorrow. They are sacrificing tomorrow for today in terms of investment, leadership, training, human capital, and commitment.

The Tomcat Group was established to help other organizations businesses improve or accelerate their performance. I see a need (or a niche) to bring proven and successful tools, guidance, experience, and assistance to others. In today's business environment, there is too much emphasis and reward placed on just making the monthly financial numbers and we have all felt the fallout with recent Wall Street bailouts, Ponzi Schemes, and the near collapse of the global financial system in 2008. I want to show businesses how they can still make the numbers and *Move Forward* without all the pain, suffering, and chaos by following a simple, proven, and structured approach or process.

Without these fundamental building blocks the organization is either going to regress to lower levels, or to lower than anticipated levels, or is not going to *Move Forward*. We must put the foundations in place today if we expect to build upon them and be successful tomorrow. This book can help.

Throughout my career and with each new challenge and opportunity, I have noticed many parallels between military operations and what is necessary for a business to run successfully. In the military you operate within a rather structured environment. There is a plan for almost everything that takes place. There is the big, overall plan, and then there are the individual support unit plans that act as sub-objectives supporting the overall plan. Everyone knows their place and the objective, what their part is within the plan, and how their piece supports and contributes to the overall plan. This can also be said for running a successful business. There is a process or structure for doing business, and each person knows what responsibility they hold in relation to the big picture or plan. Patton said it very clearly: "The soldier must know his objective and what he's doing at all times." This is true for businesses as well.

Of course, nothing ever goes exactly to plan every time, and we always end up adjusting the plan to meet the objective. As in a military operation, whether it's weather-related, somebody's not where they're supposed to be, or other issues that crop up along the way, adjustments need to be made when necessary. The key is in recognizing when a change needs to be made and making the change in order to continue to *Move Forward!* As George S. Patton stated, "Strategy and tactics do not change. Only the means of applying them is different." This also holds true in business. Things change and we must adapt our means or tactics to support the plan and lead it through to a successful conclusion.

In the military everyone is striving toward and focused on attaining the overall objective. Everyone is going in the same direction, and that direction is clear. In addition, there is a strong sense of *esprit de corps* focused upon attaining that objective. Everyone is operating together in unison, and it should be the same within a business. In business today we also need to be structured in our approach to leading our organizations. Just as in the military, these plans provide the organization the direction it needs. Without them, the organization is just a wandering generality.

The idea of setting a direction and establishing a plan similar to that of a military operation is not necessarily unique. In fact, I think a lot of people understand the need, but in this downturned economy, we have become so focused on meeting the short term financials that the overall concept and purpose of where the business is going gets lost in the process.

Additionally, in order to cut costs, quite a few businesses have eliminated important and experienced talent. I watched a company replace key leaders with younger, less experienced managers making 35-50% less than the experienced people they replaced. It may seem like an immediate fix and it works very well in the short term, but the company is now suffering due to the lack of experience in critical positions. The business has become stagnant and has even declined. Morale, efficiencies, employee turnover (even more would leave if the job market would pick up), and customer service are suffering. Again, I think business leaders see the issue, but they are so focused on making the short term financial numbers, they don't want to or can't acknowledge it themselves. They are in the short term survival mode. They have sacrificed their future by simply cutting the dollars to improve the bottom line. They have attacked it from the wrong side.

What I've learned in my career is that by establishing the direction and taking a straightforward, basic, simple, no-nonsense approach to business, you can *Go Forward* and *Accelerate Performance*. This same simple and structured approach was used by General George S. Patton in WWII. It worked for him, and I've found that the same approach works in business as well.

Over the past 20 years, I have read every book I could find regarding General Patton. To date, my personal library has over 35 books written about him and his experiences both before and during WWII. I have traveled to many sites important to Patton throughout his life and career, including the family burial plot in San Marino, California, the church where he married his wife, Beatrice, his home at Green Meadows north of Boston and the Desert Training Center near Indio, California and where he made his famous Knutsford speech. I've been fascinated and intrigued with the man, who he was, and his accomplishments. And, as a result of my interest, I have discovered that the same philosophies, concepts, and tactics Patton applied to war are applicable in today's business world.

MY

GET  REWARD

1

CHAPTER 2
MEET THE GENERAL

"L'audace, l'audace, toujours l'audace."
("Audacity, audacity, always audacity.")

Gen. George S. Patton
(Taken from Frederick the Great)

This book was not meant to be a thorough and comprehensive biography of General George S. Patton. That is not its intent or purpose. There have been several comprehensive and well written books such as *The Patton Papers* by Martin Blumenson, *A Genius for War* by Carlo De Este, and *Patton* by Ladislas Farago that contain a much deeper look at Patton and his life.

This book was written to highlight Patton's philosophies and concepts and to illustrate how those same ideas, thoughts, processes, and mindsets can be utilized to *Go Forward* and *Accelerate Performance* in today's business world.

This chapter provides a general overview of Patton, highlighting some of his background and career. In most cases, key aspects of his operations will be discussed later in the book.

Patton's Famous Speech (Taken from the Patton Society website: Charles M. Province)

This speech was made by Patton on June 5, 1944 the day before the Allied invasion of Europe. This is the original speech, which gives a good look at the man who was General George S. Patton and provides insights into his philosophies.

"Men, this stuff that some sources sling around about America wanting out of this war, not wanting to fight, is a crock of bullshit. Americans love to fight, traditionally. All real Americans love the sting and clash of battle. You are here today for three reasons. First, because you are here to defend your homes and your loved ones. Second, you are here for your own self respect, because you would not want to be anywhere else. Third, you are here because you are real men and all real men like to fight. When you, here, everyone of you, were kids, you all admired the champion marble player, the fastest runner, the toughest boxer, the big league ball players, and the All-American football players. Americans

love a winner. Americans will not tolerate a loser. Americans despise cowards. Americans play to win all of the time. I wouldn't give a hoot in hell for a man who lost and laughed. That's why Americans have never lost nor will ever lose a war; for the very idea of losing is hateful to an American."

"You are not all going to die. Only two percent of you right here today would die in a major battle. Death must not be feared. Death, in time, comes to all men. Yes, every man is scared in his first battle. If he says he's not, he's a liar. Some men are cowards but they fight the same as the brave men or they get the hell slammed out of them watching men fight who are just as scared as they are. The real hero is the man who fights even though he is scared. Some men get over their fright in a minute under fire. For some, it takes an hour. For some, it takes days. But a real man will never let his fear of death overpower his honor, his sense of duty to his country, and his innate manhood. Battle is the most magnificent competition in which a human being can indulge. It brings out all that is best and it removes all that is base. Americans pride themselves on being He Men and they ARE He Men. Remember that the enemy is just as frightened as you are, and probably more so. They are not supermen."

"All through your Army careers, you men have bitched about what you call 'chicken shit drilling.' That, like everything else in this Army, has a definite purpose. That purpose is alertness. Alertness must be bred into every soldier. I don't give a fuck for a man who's not always on his toes. You men are veterans or you wouldn't be here. You are ready for what's to come. A man must be alert at all times if he expects to stay alive. If you're not alert, sometime, a German son-of-an-asshole-bitch is going to sneak up behind you and beat you to death with a sock full of shit!" The men roared in agreement.

"There are four hundred neatly marked graves somewhere in Sicily. All because one man went to sleep on the job. But they are German graves, because we caught the bastard asleep before they did. An Army is a team. It lives, sleeps, eats, and fights as a team. This individual heroic stuff is pure horse shit. The bilious bastards who write that kind of stuff for the Saturday Evening Post don't know any more about real fighting under fire than they know about fucking!"

"We have the finest food, the finest equipment, the best spirit, and the best men in the world, Why, by God, I actually pity those poor sons-of-bitches we're going up against. By God, I do."

"My men don't surrender. I don't want to hear of any soldier under my command being captured unless he has been hit. Even if you are hit, you can still fight back. That's not just bull shit either. The kind of man that I want in my command is just like the lieutenant in Libya, who, with a Luger against his chest, jerked off his helmet, swept the gun aside with one hand, and busted the hell out of the Kraut with his helmet. Then he jumped on the gun and went out and killed another German before they knew what the hell was coming off. And, all of that time, this man had a bullet through a lung. There was a real man!"

"All of the real heroes are not storybook combat fighters, either. Every single man in this Army plays a vital role. Don't ever let up. Don't ever think that your job is unimportant. Every man has a job to do and he must do it. Every man is a vital link in the great chain. What if every truck driver suddenly decided that he didn't like the whine of those shells overhead, turned yellow, and jumped headlong into a ditch? The cowardly bastard could say, 'Hell, they won't miss me, just one man in thousands.' But, what if every man thought that way? Where in the hell would we be now? What would our country, our loved ones, our homes, even the world, be like? No, God damn it, Americans don't think like that. Every man does his job. Every man serves the whole. Every department, every unit, is important in the vast scheme of this war. The ordnance men are needed to supply the guns and machinery of war to keep us rolling. The Quartermaster is needed to bring up food and clothes because where we are going there isn't a hell of a lot to steal. Every last man on K.P. has a job to do, even the one who heats our water to keep us from getting the 'G.I. Shits.'"

"Each man must not think only of himself, but also of his buddy fighting beside him. We don't want yellow cowards in this Army. They should be killed off like rats. If not, they will go home after this war and breed more cowards. The brave men will breed more brave men. Kill off the God damned cowards and we will have a nation of brave men. One of the bravest men that I ever saw was *a fellow on top of a telegraph pole in the midst of a furious fire fight in Tunisia. I stopped and asked what the hell he was doing up there at a time like that. He answered, 'Fixing the wire, Sir.' I asked, 'Isn't that a little unhealthy right about now?' He answered, 'Yes Sir, but the God damned wire has to be fixed.' I asked, 'Don't those planes strafing the road bother you?' And he answered, 'No, Sir, but you sure as hell do!' Now, there was a real man. A real soldier. There was a man who devoted all he had to his duty, no matter how seemingly insignificant his duty might appear at the time, no matter how great the odds. And you should have seen those trucks on the road to Tunisia. Those drivers were magnificent. All day and all night they rolled over those son-of-a-bitching roads, never stopping, never faltering from their course, with shells bursting all around them all of the time. We got through on good old American guts. Many of those men drove for over forty consecutive hours. These men weren't combat men, but they were soldiers with a job to do. They did it, and in one hell of a way they did it. They were part of a team. Without team effort, without them, the fight would have been lost. All of the links in the chain pulled together and the chain became unbreakable."*

"Don't forget you men don't know that I'm here. No mention of that fact is to be made in any letters. The world is not supposed to know what the hell happened to me. I'm not supposed to be commanding this Army. I'm not even supposed to be here in England. Let the first bastards to find out be the Goddamned Germans. Some day I want to see them raise up on their piss-soaked hind legs and howl, 'Jesus Christ, it's the God damned Third Army again and that son-of-a-fucking-bitch Patton.'"

"We want to get the hell over there the quicker we clean up this God damned mess, the quicker we can take a little jaunt against the purple pissing Japs and clean out their nest, too. Before the Goddamned Marines get all of the credit."

"Sure, we want to go home. We want this war over with. The quickest way to get it over with is to go get the bastards who started it. The quicker they are whipped, the quicker we can go home. The shortest way home is through Berlin and Tokyo. And when we get to Berlin, I am personally going to shoot that paper hanging son-of-a-bitch Hitler. Just like I'd shoot a snake!"

"When a man is lying in a shell hole, if he just stays there all day, a German will get to him eventually. The hell with that idea. The hell with taking it. My men don't dig foxholes. I don't want them to. Foxholes only slow up an offensive. Keep moving. And don't give the enemy time to dig one either. We'll win this war, but we'll win it only by fighting and by showing the Germans that we've got more guts than they have; or ever will have. We're not going to just shoot the sons-of-bitches, we're going to rip out their living God damned guts and use them to grease the treads of our tanks. We're going to murder those lousy Hun cocksuckers by the bushel-fucking-basket. War is a bloody, killing business. You've got to spill their blood, or they will spill yours. Rip them up the belly. Shoot them in the guts. When shells are hitting all around you and you wipe the dirt off your face and realize that instead of dirt it's the blood and guts of what once was your best friend beside you, you'll know what to do!"

"I don't want to get any messages saying, 'I am holding my position.' We are not holding a God damned thing. Let the Germans do that. We are advancing constantly and we are not interested in holding onto anything, except the enemy's balls. We are going to twist his balls and kick the living shit out of him all of the time. Our basic plan of operation is to advance and to keep on advancing regardless of whether we have to go over, under, or through the enemy. We are going to go through him like crap through a goose; like shit through a tin horn!"

"From time to time there will be some complaints that we are pushing our people too hard. I don't give a good God damn about such complaints. I believe in the old and sound rule that an ounce of sweat will save a gallon of blood. The harder we push, the more Germans we will kill. The more Germans we kill, the fewer of our men will be killed. Pushing means fewer casualties. I want you all to remember that."

"There is one great thing that you men will all be able to say after this war is over and you are home once again. You may be thankful that twenty years from now when you are sitting by the fireplace with your grandson on your knee and he asks you what you did in the great World War II, you WON'T have to *cough, shift him to the other knee and say, 'Well, your Granddaddy shoveled shit in Louisiana.' No, Sir, you can look him straight in the eye and say, "Son, your Granddaddy rode with the Great Third Army and a Son-of-a-Goddamned-Bitch named Georgie Patton!"*

General George S. Patton was one of the great leaders of WWII, and a very complicated individual. He was an American hero, but was also a person of controversy. He was outspoken, well read, a historian, profane, accident prone, self-driven, a skilled marksman, a polo player, had high expectations for himself and his troops, but he was also religious, wrote poetry, and believed in reincarnation.

Patton was focused on being a winner and would do whatever it took to win, driving himself hard. Everything had a purpose; everything had a plan. While portrayed as a hard charging, ruthless leader, he also suffered from internal feelings of self-doubt and at times did not feel he was good enough. Today we would call that an inferiority complex or a poor self image. As a result, he would routinely question his abilities, but at the same time pushed himself to succeed, striving to be a winner.

George "Georgie" Smith Patton, Jr. was born November 11, 1885, to an affluent family of Scottish decent and raised in San Gabriel Township, California, which is now the city of San Marino, with his parents, sister Nita, and Aunt Nannie. His father, George Smith Patton, Sr., was a prominent lawyer and politician, and his mother, Ruth Wilson, kept house. Patton looked up to his father and was always seeking his approval. Some say that the need for his father's approval is what gave Patton his drive to excel. Aunt Nannie functioned as a surrogate mother for George and spent considerable time reading and educating him during his childhood. Georgie was home schooled by his father and Aunt Nannie until the age of 11, and due to his dyslexia, struggled with mathematics and spelling.

Having come from a long line of soldiers who fought in the Revolutionary, Mexican, and Civil Wars, Patton from an early age became fascinated with history, especially military history. Patton's father and Aunt Nannie would tell young Georgie stories of his military ancestors and of their heroism and glory. These stories spurred the desire for Patton to become a military leader and hero in his own right.

In 1903, Patton attended the Virginia Military Institute and then, through some intervention by his father, received an appointment to the United States Military Academy at West Point, where he was required to repeat his first year because of poor academic performance in mathematics. However, Patton did not give up; he pushed himself hard to overcome the obstacle. At West Point, Patton was not well liked by his peers and was viewed as an arrogant loaner who was not a team player. However, this was by Patton's design. Patton kept constant journals, often writing about what he thought it took to be a strong military leader. Those thoughts and beliefs were carried with him not just through West Point, but throughout his career. In 1909, Patton graduated from West Point ranking 46 out of 103 and received a commission as a 2nd Lieutenant in the Cavalry. During most of Patton's time at West Point either his mother or Aunt Nannie lived nearby, providing support.

Patton competed in the 1912 Stockholm Olympics in the first modern Pentathlon. During the pistol shooting portion of the event, there was a dispute amongst the officials. The judges determined that one of Patton's rounds had missed the target. Patton responded by stating that the holes in the paper target from the previous shots were so large that his shots passed right through them. The controversy regarding Patton's shots continued on, but ultimately the judges' decision was upheld and Patton placed fifth overall in the event. Patton qualified for the U.S. Modern Pentathlon team again for the 1916 Summer Olympics, which were to be held in Berlin, Germany, but these Olympics were cancelled due to the outbreak of World War I.

After the Olympics, Patton paid his own way and studied for a time in France. He wanted to become a great swordsman, and at the time the best place to learn was at the Calvary School of Saumur. It was during these two trips to France that Patton first saw the French countryside that would become such a large part of his life 30 years later as he led the 3rd Army's drive across France.

He excelled in fencing, and later became the Army's youngest soldier to earn "Master of the Sword" at Ft. Riley Kansas. Patton also advised the Ordnance Department on sword redesign and improved and modernized the Army's fencing techniques.

In 1913 George S. Patton married Beatrice Ayer. Beatrice was the daughter of a wealthy industrialist and business owner near Boston, Massachusetts. She and Patton had been childhood sweethearts, and she visited him several times in California while he was in his teens, and while he was studying at West Point. They made their home north of Boston at Green Meadows Farm in Hamilton, Massachusetts raising three children, Beatrice, Ruth Ellen, and George. Beatrice was devoted to her husband, assisted him in his endeavors, and was very protective of him, his reputation, and image. She was his strongest advocate and supporter. She also published *Blood of the Shark, A Romance of Early Hawaii*. She died of an aortic aneurysm in 1953, and her ashes were spread across her husband's grave by their children.

In 1916 Patton and General John J. Pershing pursued Pancho Villa on the U.S.-Mexico border near El Paso as part of the U.S. Punitive Expedition. These were Patton's first official experiences in battle.

At the beginning of WWI, Captain Patton launched and then commanded the U.S. Light Tank Training school at Bourg, France. He desperately wanted more battle experience and believed that in the tank corps, he would have a greater opportunity to get it. Patton commanded American tanks in several major offensives. On September 26, 1918, he was wounded in the left thigh and buttocks near the town of Cheppy. While recuperating from his injuries, the war ended with the armistice of November 11, 1918, which was also Patton's 33rd birthday.

MY

GET

REWARD

2

During both WWI and WWII Patton took great pride in exhibiting calmness under fire. While in battle, he refused to flinch, jump, or dive into a foxhole, believing that this was a sign of great courage and demonstrated that strong leadership included not showing fear under fire.

Between WWI and WWII he held positions in Washington, D.C. and Hawaii. He also successfully sailed his own schooner, *Acturus*, from San Francisco, California to Hawaii. This was a great accomplishment for Patton as he continually struggled with mathematics (due to his dyslexia), which was critical in the use of a sextant and course plotting.

Just prior to America's entry into WWII, Patton was given orders to the newly established U.S. Army Desert Training Camp located near Indio, California. Patton believed that if soldiers were going to fight in the desert, they needed to understand how to live, fight, and survive under the harsh desert conditions. He insisted that every person under his command spend at least six weeks at the desert training center before being sent to North Africa.

Over the course of WWII, Patton commanded the Western Tank Force as part of Operation Torch, which was the first all U.S. push into North Africa. While in North Africa he took command of the U.S. II Corps after their defeat at Kasserine Pass, quickly turning the organization around defeating the Germans at El Guettar a short time later.

Commanding the U.S. 7th Army in Sicily, he and his men were charged with to protecting the western side of the British 8th Army as they advanced towards Messina. Patton was not pleased with the assignment and devised his own plan to prove the value and capability of the U.S. soldier. We will discuss this later.

In the months before the Normandy invasion, Patton was assigned to take command of the fictional First U.S. Army Group (FUSAG). At the time the Germans were convinced that Patton was going to lead the European invasion and the allies wanted to build on that perception.

Patton then took command of the U.S. 3rd Army shortly after D-Day in early August of 1944. As part of Operation Cobra, his 3rd Army began its push out of Normandy and then pushed aggressively eastward across France. Patton was relentless in his drive and had made major progress in a very short time. However, with the rapid advance, he outran his supply lines and was pushing out beyond the Allied front lines. For a time, Patton and his 3rd Army were held back.

In late 1944 (six months after D-Day) the Germans had launched a major surprise offensive in the area of the Ardennes in northeastern France, Belgium, and Luxembourg that became known as the Battle of the Bulge. During the course of this battle, the U.S. 101st Airborne was trapped at Bastogne and Patton and his 3rd Army executed a successful, well performed, and highly aggressive rescue operation.

After WWII in October 1945, Patton, now a full general, took command of the U.S. 15th Army, which was tasked with occupational issues and in the writing of historical data related to the war in Europe. Patton was not happy about losing his beloved 3rd Army and being relegated to writing history.

At this point in his career, Patton's intent was to go home for the holidays and in January, 1946 to either resign or retire. He wasn't sure which, but he was fed up, frustrated, and felt it was time to leave the military. However, on December 9, 1945, just a day before he was to leave for the United States, Patton and his chief of staff, Major General Hobart R. "Hap" Gay, were on hunting trip outside Mannheim, Germany. Their Cadillac had stopped at a railroad crossing to wait for a passing train. After the train passed, Patton's car began to move forward, and a military two and a half ton truck turned in front of them. Patton's car was only going about 15 miles per hour, but upon impact he was launched forward where he sliced his scalp on the dome light and knocked his head into the partition separating the driver in the front from the passengers in the back. This caused a fractured vertebra, which resulted in Patton being paralyzed from the neck down. Patton was the only person injured in the accident. The Army flew senior level surgeons from the U.S. to

Germany to care for him. However, on December 21, 1945, Patton died from an embolism as a result of complications from his accident. He died at the age of 60, and at the time had a son attending West Point.

Patton is buried at the Luxembourg American Cemetery and Memorial in Hamm, Luxembourg along with other members of the 3rd Army, which is what he wanted. He wanted to be with his men. On March 19, 1947, his body was moved from the original grave site in the cemetery to its current prominent location at the head of his former troops, as an honor to his belief that a good leader should be seen and lead from the front.

Gravesite of General George S. Patton at Hamm, Luxemburg

A memorial to Patton was placed at the Wilson-Patton family plot at the San Gabriel Cemetery in San Gabriel, California, adjacent to the Church of Our Savior where Patton was baptized and confirmed. At the church is a stained glass window that features a picture of him riding in a tank. A statue of General Patton is between the church and the family plot.

General George S. Patton was the type of man people either loved or hated, there was no in between. He had the audacity to speak up and the courage to be outspoken when others around him were silent. Sometimes his words were positive, sometimes negative, and sometimes they got him into trouble. He was loyal to the causes and people he believed in and was never afraid to stand up for those beliefs, whether they were popular or not, and above all he was loyal to his men.

After World War II vets would frequently be asked, "What outfit were you with during the war?" Most would respond by stating their unit number with a phrase such as "I was with the 8th Air Force." But those who were under the command of General Patton would proudly say, "I was with Patton." That itself is a tribute to the man, his leadership, and his accomplishments.

CHAPTER 3
PATTON ON LEADERSHIP

"Leadership is the thing that wins battles, I have it–but I'll be damned if I can define it. Probably it consists in knowing what you want to do and doing it and getting mad if anyone steps in the way. Self confidence and leadership are brothers."

General George S. Patton

You can't write a book about General George S. Patton without having a chapter on leadership. Patton's leadership style was simple, direct, and no nonsense. It fostered trust, respect, and success for him and set his expectations for the troops under his command.

Consider his most popular campaigns.

OPERATION TORCH, MOROCCO

In November 1942, Patton was part of Operation Torch, the Allied invasion of northern Africa under the command of Gen. Eisenhower (U.S.) and Field Marshall Alexander (British) with 102 ships and 70,000 troops, including 24,000 under Patton. His objective was to capture Casablanca.

On November 9, Patton noted in his diary that during the landings on the beach he found it to be in total chaos. The landing area had been strafed and bombed; none of the material was moving off the beach, and none of the officers were taking command. The situation was such a mess that Patton personally took charge of the beach activities and attempted to get things in order and under control even to the point of personally directing traffic on the beach.

This event highlights the need for leaders, not only in the military but also in business, to take charge of situations, issues, or problems and get them under control, structured, and flowing. Of particular interest for me is the fact that the officers on the beach were not taking charge of this situation. I've seen managers (note that I did not say leaders) do the same thing in business. Things are going astray in one or more areas inside their departments and no one is taking charge and getting it on back on track. They just stand idly by letting it all happen, knowing that it isn't right. Patton's comment, "We have many commanders, but few leaders," fits this business scenario very well and I've seen it too many times.

This case also highlights Patton's desire to be where the action is (in business that would be out on the shop floor) and his willingness to roll up his sleeves and get dirty to get the situation under control. He exhibited strong leadership traits under fire by getting things *Moving Forward* and *Accelerating the Performance* on the beach. We need more of this in the upper, middle, and lower levels of our businesses. We need Leaders in our organization. Not Managers. And there is a difference.

II CORPS, NORTH AFRICA

Patton took over command of II Corps in early March 1943 after they took heavy losses in the battle for Kasserine Pass in Tunisia. Replacing Gen. Lloyd Fredendall, he found the outfit to be undisciplined, unkempt, untrained, and unmotivated. Fredendall had a completely different leadership style than Patton, and Eisenhower thought Patton had the leadership skills and traits necessary to whip II Corps into shape and reinstill pride in themselves and their unit. Ike was right.

Patton immediately began to make changes and it started with simple things such as enforcement of uniform regulations and hefty fines for things such as not wearing a helmet, no tie, no leggings, not shaving or having a non-military haircut. Patton's "Back to Basics" campaign quickly began to instill the discipline, unity, pride, and teamwork amongst the troops. Although Patton was not popular with his discipline and fines program, the troops of II Corps gained respect for Patton and felt that with Patton, they had a better chance for success in battle. They also felt inspired and motivated to have someone of such stature and reputation leading them in battle. Patton's philosophy of "Leadership is not a popularity contest" demonstrates this concept. This discipline campaign paid off several weeks later when Patton's II Corps met and defeated the Germans at El Guettar.

From a business leader perspective, I think the knowledge to be gained here is that leading a simple "Back to Basics" approach to business can pay off very well. In business today, this simple "Back to Basics" approach can easily start with arriving to work on time, in the appropriate dress, getting to meetings on time, completing tasks on time, setting the expectations, and being held accountable for their performance—an uncomfortable and at times and impossible task today.

OPERATION HUSKY: 7TH ARMY, SICILY

After his success with II Corps in Tunisia, Patton was given command of the 7th Army and was part of Operation Husky, which was a joint U.S. and British invasion of Sicily under the command of General Eisenhower.

Patton made a devoted effort to show that the American soldiers were better than they were perceived to be by the British. In typical Patton "leading from the front" fashion, after the landings in Sicily he was running around in jeeps, command cars, and aircraft visiting each Army unit and motivating, coaching, and leading the men toward their objective. He was spending as much as 20 hours a day among the troops driving himself, his commanders, and troops to go beyond what was expected of them.

This passionate and persistent effort demonstrates an extremely strong level of commitment as a leader. Patton was going beyond the normal day-to-day general activities, doing more than what was expected. He lived by his quote to "Do more than is required of you." Business leaders can learn from this mindset. Being a successful leader today means having the commitment, engagement, drive, excitement, and passion to take your organization to the next level of *Accelerated Performance* and *Go Forward*. It is no nine to five job. To be successful you have to be seen by your staff and employees and be willing to go the extra mile with them in regards to commitment, dedication, devotion, and passion. As a leader, you need to lead the effort.

BATTLE OF THE BULGE

In December 1944, the Germans mounted a large offensive in the Ardennes area of Belgium. This offensive was quietly prepared with the objective being to break through the Allied lines and capture the port of Antwerp, thus cutting off the Allied supply lines. By late December the offensive was in full swing and the Germans had the U.S. 101st surrounded at Bastogne, a major intersection with seven main roads going in and out. Conditions at this time were poor for the 101st as ammunition, food, and supplies were low.

General Eisenhower held a meeting in Verdun on December 19 with Patton, Bradley, and several other staff officers. When asked when he could attack, Patton committed to attacking in 48 hours. This created a major stir as some thought the plan and timing were too aggressive. Patton knew it was aggressive, but had confidence in his men and felt strongly that it could be accomplished. He knew what they were capable of and knew they were up to the task.

To accomplish the task Patton had to shift his current easterly advance 90 degrees to the north and move his troops 100 miles. This posed huge logistical issues, compounded by the fact it was the middle of winter. This was a major move.

On December 22, Patton began his attack as promised, relieving the 101st on December 26. This was a major victory and triumph for Patton and his 3rd Army.

This event highlights the aggressive, passionate, and committed leadership attributes of Patton. He took on the hard and complicated task of getting to Bastogne and rescuing the 101st. He created and communicated the vision, developed the strategy and worked the alignment and action plans with his staff to make it happen. Had it not been for Patton's energy, drive, and leadership, the results in Bastogne would have been very different for the Allies.

Business leaders can easily learn from this event. To me it illustrates that any difficult and seemingly unattainable goal can be met by communicating the vision, developing the strategy, and leading the way in the execution of that strategy. Granted, the severity of the issues in Bastogne was much more intense, but the simple principles applied by Patton can be used in business to solve our own problems.

Patton was a complicated man and his leadership style was a mix of many attributes, both good and bad. Early in his career, in 1909, Patton wrote in one of his West Point notebooks what he thought it took to be a great general. Those qualities were:

- Tactically Aggressive (Loves a fight)
- Strength of Character
- Steadiness of Purpose
- Acceptance of Responsibility
- Energy
- Good Health and Strength

Patton understood then what it meant to be a leader living and functioning under these attributes all through his life. Today, many businesses and government agencies, as well as many leaders, are missing some of these qualities.

Patton had the image in the media of "Old Blood and Guts" and being a tough, demanding, and "Hard Charging" leader. At times his actions seemed almost reckless, but in reality most of this was actually an act. Everything Patton did was calculated and well thought out and he was thoroughly devoted to the task at hand. Everything he did had a plan and a purpose. Patton was known to repeat a quote from Napoleon stating that "To command an Army well a general must think of nothing else." He functioned under that premise.

Patton was an actor and portrayed the part of a warrior right down to the "war face" that he practiced in the mirror and displayed in public, using it to motivate not only himself but also his troops.

Patton set high expectations for himself and excelled at every task both from a personal and military perspective. He wanted to win and would push himself and lead his troops on the path to win. He was quoted as stating, "America loves a winner, and will not tolerate a loser; this is why America has never, and will never lose a war."

He drove himself hard and as a result he drove others to accelerated levels of performance. He also functioned under the concept that "Lack of orders is not an excuse for inaction." We seem to miss this aspect in business today. Many managers today wait for someone to tell them what to do. They lack the ownership, responsibility, and leadership to take command.

Patton had a strong passion and drive for what he believed in and was committed to that passion. He was outspoken with thoughts, beliefs, and convictions and proudly stood behind them. As a result, there was no doubt what his thoughts were on a particular subject. In some cases that outspokenness got him in trouble, but he spoke his mind nonetheless. This outspokenness and ability to take a stand is often lost today in our politically correct business environments.

In his world, Patton always had a plan for everything and in most cases a plan B. Nothing was ever left to chance.

He had somewhat of a simplistic approach to planning and meeting objectives. His thoughts were that plans should be simple to understand, communicate, and execute. They should not be changed once they were put in motion, as changing plans would result in confusion and progress. His sayings that "One must choose a system and stick to it," and that the "Strategy and tactics do not change, only the means of applying them is different" highlight that premise as well as his assertion that "Plans should be simple and never changed." How many times in business do the strategies turn into the "flavor of the month" as objectives and priorities change in a relatively short period of time? We as leaders need to have the courage and confidence in ourselves to set a direction and stay the course.

Patton stated that "Leadership was not a popularity contest." He had a deep admiration for his troops, cared for them and spoke openly about their accomplishments, and always gave credit where credit was due. He was proud of them and spent a considerable amount of time amongst them. He was comfortable with them and knew that they were the ones that made him successful. He set the direction and the troops put it into action and executed it. Leading from the front, Patton knew that without the respect and support from his troops, he was not going to be successful in battle and thus fall short of his objective. As he said, "Lead, do not rule over your troops." In most cases, he had their respect and was often referred to as "Georgie" amongst his troops.

Patton had a strong ability to inspire his men through his public speaking. He was highly visible. He was larger than life and a charismatic speaker who was continually communicating his path, thoughts, and ideas as well as inspiring his troops while in front of them. He was in his element when speaking to them, like an actor on stage. He talked to them on their level and used their language right down to the profanity. Through his speaking and constantly being out amongst the troops, everyone knew where he was going.

"A piece of spaghetti or a military unit can only be led from the front end. A general can't push it from behind, but has to be up front pulling it." He always led from the front and was uncomfortable in the rear areas, feeling that all good leaders needed to be seen by their troops providing inspiration and motivation. This was a leadership trait he firmly believed in and insisted that his officers did the same. And he was a firm believer that the more senior you were, the more time you had available and as such he expected you to spend more time with the troops and go up to the front and lead. Because he was always amongst the troops, Patton had a handle on the situation, all the while leading, inspiring, and communicating what the objective was and where they were going and offering his guidance along the way. As business leaders we need to be up front as well and not buried in our offices or conference rooms.

He believed in teams and said an "Army is a team…" He was able to align his troops and their actions in order to get everyone going in the same direction. This was a key element to his success. In his outfit, everyone knew what was going on and what they needed to do. And they all wanted to be a part of it.

Patton set the expectations for those under his command and those expectations were high. He expected them to perform and there was no doubt that they would be held accountable for that performance. There was never any doubt where you stood with Patton.

Patton also believed that "Every leader must have the authority to match his responsibility." He had an innate ability to innovate, inspire, and lead change and could easily inspire a team approach to address a problem or issue and then motivate and lead that team to success. He constantly studied history and leadership in order to learn from it and was able to apply that learning. This understanding of history contributed to his ability to develop strategies and tactics. Patton said, "Do everything you ask of those you command" and would never ask anyone to do anything he wouldn't do. He was a hands-on leader and was not afraid to get dirty.

He was very committed to the task at hand and did everything in his capacity and ability to follow it through. This was quite evident in both his drive across France and his efforts at Bastogne during the Battle of the Bulge. He was decisive and had a very strong ability to assess the information in front of him and then make good, sound, and well thought out decisions. This was a key trait of being a great leader and was developed through reading, training, and experience. As a result, when the time came, he instinctively knew what to do.

Patton also had a soft and compassionate side. During the war he was always visiting field hospitals where his troops were recovering from their wounds. There are numerous accounts of Patton becoming very emotional during these visits and in some cases he was speechless and reduced to tears. He felt that if he had been a better leader, these troops would not have been wounded.

He possessed a strong character. Even during battle, Patton strived to maintain his personal calm in order to demonstrate to his troops his courage while inspiring them to fight and combat their fears. Patton believed that "Courage was fear holding on one moment longer."

To sum up Patton, he:

- Had a straightforward and a no-nonsense leadership style
- Led from the front
- Was inspirational
- Was accountable
- Was visible
- Had a plan for almost everything he did
- Was decisive
- Was committed
- Was action oriented
- Took educated and calculated risks
- Had a compassionate, soft side
- Made the effort to know his human, equipment, and logistics resource strengths, weaknesses, capacity, and limitations
- Had a strong sense of teamwork
- Had no political aspirations: What you saw is what you got

Patton has been singled out as a great leader for his ability to inspire his troops and for their ability to do great things, as was the case during his campaigns in North Africa, Sicily, France, and Belgium. He was a charismatic, flamboyant, and outspoken leader who drove himself and his troops to excel in everything they did. Patton was a winner in everything he did, from polo matches to combat.

Patton was not a stereotypical soldier and stood out as a result. Well known as someone who could get things moving in a short period of time, he was always being given difficult assignments and excelled at all of them. A strong communicator, he knew where he was going and expressed it all the time and surrounded himself with good, solid performers, stood back and let them do their jobs. But he also set the expectations and held them accountable for their performance. As a leader he was proud of his team and praised them often. He packaged and sold himself to his troops, peers, superiors, and the public.

For a more modern leadership comparison, General Norman "Stormin' Normin" Schwarzkopf was the Commander of the Coalition Forces in the Persian Gulf War in 1991. Schwarzkopf developed and executed his plan during the Gulf War, ending it in just 431 days and with minimal casualties.

Like Patton, Schwarzkopf was also viewed as a strong leader and tough commander who nevertheless cared for his troops and their well-being both in the Persian Gulf War and during his time in Vietnam. Like Patton, he also had the respect and loyalty of his troops and was often amongst them working even in times of crisis, such as during a minefield incident in Vietnam where Schwarzkopf personally put himself in danger to rescue his troops.

Schwartzkopf's famous quote of "When you get on that plane to go home, if the last thing you think about me is 'I hate that son of a bitch,' then that is fine because you're going home alive" speaks volumes of how he cared for and felt about his men.

Another great leader that exhibited strong leadership qualities reminiscent of Patton was President John F. Kennedy. JFK was a young, good looking, and charismatic speaker and communicator who spoke to the American public in terms they understood.

He had a vision for this country and expressed it openly at every opportunity. His vision included keeping our country safe, putting a man on the moon before the Soviets, the Civil Rights Movement, establishment of the Peace Corps, and a healthy focus on education, technology, and health. He knew where he wanted to lead America, communicated it, followed through, and rallied the American people around that vision.

JFK was a Navy PT Boat Commander in the Pacific during WWII and was wounded during the war. He was an advocate of people working together to improve this country and he instilled a strong sense of patriotism along the way. He knew where he wanted to take America.

His image of wholesome family values and Camelot generated a strong bond with the American public. During the Cuban Missile Crisis, JFK showed extreme courage and took a strong stance with the Soviets and brought us to the brink of war. But through his strong charismatic leadership, communication, and compassion for the American people, he succeeded against the Soviets and they withdrew.

President Ronald Reagan was another great leader who had the decisiveness and courage to take a stand. His foreign policy stands out. Essentially, how he handled the arms race with the Soviet Union, the Air Traffic Controllers' strike, and the U.S. airstrike in Libya against terrorist camps operating openly during the high point of Gadhafi's reign, speaks volumes about taking a stand in the midst of turmoil.

This fits well with Patton's philosophy that "you need to overcome the tug of people against you as you reach for high goals," and "The results prove that, as ever, leadership and audacity bring success."

President Franklin Roosevelt led this country during two of its worst crises—the Great Depression and WWII. His New Deal got America back on its feet after the depression in the early 1930s, using the Civilian Conservation Corps to offer jobs to the unemployed. FDR kept America focused and continually communicated with the public through his Fireside Chats. He communicated his agenda, was committed to it, and obtained the needed support and we reaped the results. His success was due to his vision, backbone, and commitment and because he was unafraid to take a stand and follow through.

Ask yourself this question: Where are the strong, no-nonsense political leaders, who take a stand and make a real difference today?

These principles work. During my career I've applied many of them and have had great success in my business turnaround situations. Patton's military leadership approach isn't any different than what is needed and used in businesses. In many cases, there simply was no vision, no plan and as a result, nothing *Moved Forward*.

I have found that most organizations are crying out for leadership. They want someone to set the vision, set the course, and guide them along the way. They're looking for feedback as to how they and the organization are doing. We need to communicate with them in a routine and direct manner. Not in finance speak but in their language. Patton spoke to his troops in their language. We should be doing the same.

These approaches are straightforward, simple, and basic. You don't need an MBA or PhD to put it all together and they don't cost big money to put into practice. By keeping it simple and continually communicating that direction or path (Read: What you want done) people will know your message and understand it, know what you want to do and where you are going, and see how their actions help the organization to get there, such as:

- If we as leaders set the example, others will follow

- Be genuine, let people see the real, caring, and understanding you

- People don't necessarily need to like you, they need to respect you

- Patton said to "say what you mean and mean what you say" and have the courage to set the course, or "one must choose a system and stick to it"

We need to adopt a simple back to basics approach to today's business issues. No potions, magic formulas, weasel words, or creative accounting. Just a simple, no nonsense plan that can be easily communicated and executed will move the organization forward, *Accelerating Performance*. It worked for Patton and I find that works in business today.

Patton knew where he was going and communicated that direction all the time to anyone who would listen. His message was simple, clear, and concise and he spoke of it in the terms his troops understood. He sold it to them on their level. In today's business environment in many cases that vision or strategy is not there and if it is there, it's not communicated and understood and as a result, no one knows what is important. These items were keys to Patton's success and hold true in today's business world as well. Without a vision or strategy, how do you know where you are going?

By taking care of our employees, they will take care of us. With loyalty, caring, fair treatment, and ethical employment practices, they will be with you for the long haul. They are not expendable resources. Patton was a firm believer in taking care of his troops.

Keep the communication lines open in all directions within the organization. There is no need to play "I've got a secret." I've seen the game played too many times. Information is power, but only if it's shared. Communicate. Put your plan together, communicate it, rally your team around it, and lead it to success. With continual open communication, the understanding and acceptance of the message will be clear.

With the state of technology in today's business world, it's easy to just send an e-mail, text, leave a voicemail, post something on the company website, or conduct a video conference. Although these are effective tools, they should not replace direct interaction with employees. Get out there. Employees want and need to see the leader and the leadership team out amongst them. Take the time and interact with them. You'll gain a better understanding of what's happening, of them and their issues as well as developing and earning their trust and respect. Patton was out there with his troops every day and as business leaders we need to do the same if we are to be effective in *Moving Forward* and *Accelerating Performance*.

In tough times, many businesses are thrust into crisis management and chaotic environments. During WWII, Patton was also thrust into a crisis management and a chaotic environment and he employed these principles and concepts to lead his troops in battle successfully.

In many cases there is an inability to make decisions. Leaders are seen as wishy-washy and not decisive. Many leaders or managers function under the idea that they might make the wrong decision or someone might not like it and we can't upset anyone these days. We don't make decisions because we don't want to draw attention to ourselves or fear being viewed as "bucking the system." Or we back away because what really needs to take place may be viewed as not politically correct. Patton's quote of "Audacity, Audacity, Always Audacity" fits here. Have the courage and audacity to be decisive and take a stand.

Then there is the potential reality of being second guessed by the next level in the organization and losing our job. In many cases, business leaders are given the responsibility to run the business, but with little or no authority. Most if not all decisions are made at higher levels or at the corporate level.

Patton believed that in order to be successful, "Every leader must have the authority to match his responsibility." Many business leaders today don't have the courage to stand behind their convictions. They live in fear of their job, do not speak their minds, and become "yes men" as a result. In many cases, we've lost the concepts of responsibility and accountability. As Patton said, "We have a lot of commanders, but not a lot of leadership." I'll substitute the word "managers" for Patton's "commanders."

Many leaders today spend all day in the offices in front of their computers or in meetings away from the day-to-day operation where things are actually getting done. Good leaders are visible and approachable and that means making yourself available. Business leaders need to get out where the action is and spend time with their troops. As Patton said, "no good decision was ever made in a swivel chair."

In some cases employees are not treated with the respect they deserve. They are viewed as expendable resources that can be eliminated (laid off) at any point regardless of how long they've been with the organization. Respect goes both ways.

In an effort to reduce costs, many companies are removing (Read: terminating) the older experienced leaders or managers and replacing them with younger, inexperienced, and cheaper ones. Loyalty is missing in both directions. Without trust and commitment it will be difficult to *Move Forward*.

By eliminating the experienced, higher paid, and seasoned segment of the labor pool that has seen and experienced the past history of errors and poor decisions, we save on costs. But in the long run these organizations end up incurring costs that far exceed those saved by letting the seasoned veteran go. These costs are incurred by the younger and less experienced ones who make the same errors and same mistakes that the veteran learned from long ago.

We allow the short term financial gains to outweigh the longer term benefits and hold back growth and ability to *Move Forward*. Patton said it best: "Personally, I am of the opinion that older men of experience, who have smelled powder and have been wounded, are of more value than mere youthful exuberance, which has not yet been disciplined. However, I seem to be in the minority in this belief."

Today we are risk-adverse and do not have the audacity to take an aggressive, calculated, and well thought out approach to expanding our business or business development activities. Patton's advice to "Take calculated risks. That is quite different from being rash" fits this premise very well.

Many organizations have not developed the trust needed to build a strong team environment. It's a dog-eat-dog environment when the organization lacks the leadership to lead the way.

We need to listen, listen, and listen some more. Your staff, or troops, have most of the answers. Real leaders have the ability to talk with them and to use their responses to lead them down a path to a successful execution. I once heard a manager tell an employee who had just offered a suggestion that "They pay me to think and you to do, so get back to work." This manager was removed soon thereafter.

Some leaders are in it only for their own personal gain and are not committed to the future of the organization. They are in it for the big bonus payout, status, and a promotion. As a result, they end up not caring about the organizational goals or its employees, only themselves.

Some leaders micromanage every aspect of their business and employees. They do not have the faith in their team to develop a plan, take action and *Move Forward*. As such everything must come to the leader for a decision. From the smallest decisions such as what color the tile is in the lobby (or even making the decision that the tile in the lobby needs to change), to giving approval for a normal employee rate increase, to what flights a salesperson takes on a sales trip (even though it is clear in the policy). The notion that "Nothing moves around here without my say so," or the comment, "Who made that decision?" hold back the ability of the organization to *Move Forward* and *Accelerate Performance*. Give your people the authority they need to make decisions and do not second guess every decision they make.

Today we need to listen to Patton and "Never tell people how to do things. Tell them what you want done and let them surprise you with the results." We as leaders need to set the stage and culture for them to develop their own plans and follow through with their execution. You've put good people in place, now step back and let them do their jobs.

In business today we have a habit of saying one thing and doing another. We tell everyone that quality and integrity are our values, but when shipments get light and the folks upstairs want more, then it's okay to ship nonconforming product, falsify financials, and look the other way. Be honest in everything you do. As Patton stated, "Say what you mean and mean what you say." In today's world the phrase is "Walk the talk." We need to have the courage to maintain our integrity and be honest with ourselves. When it comes to integrity and character, if we don't set the example we've lost the respect of the organization, thus inhibiting its ability to *Move Forward*.

Patton believed that integrity was an important character trait for leaders. He believed that "Officers must assert themselves by example and voice," and that "In the long run, it's what we do, not what we say that will destroy us."

Remember that history has proven that principles like Patton's work. If we continue to study history we can continually learn from it without the cost of relearning from previous mistakes.

Despite the current trends moving away, there are many great modern examples of leadership. The first one that comes to mind is the Lockheed Skunk Works. This organization was given the leadership, latitude, and support to develop some fantastic aircraft. Another isn't a business success, but I think Sarah Palin has been very successful marketing herself, her vision and values. Think of Fred Smith and his leadership at FedEx, or Cessna Aircraft and its handling of the general aviation downturn. The Triumph Group, Ranger International, Duncan Aircraft, and numerous other well-run businesses fit this category as well.

If the organization is successful, there is a lot to be said for not making any major adjustments. However, if the organization is interested in *Accelerating Performance*, then they should look at Patton's principles to help it *Move Forward*.

I've seen numerous business successes that benefited from these principles. These business successes were often the result of a visionary leader who had rallied a team around his vision. This vision was well communicated and understood by all those involved and a strategy was developed in support of that vision. The leader was highly committed to that vision and strategy and had the backbone to stick to it, leading the organization to success. They are truly success stories and the success rested with the leader of the organization and the commitment to that vision.

These principles work even better when the organization picks the right, bright and forward thinking leadership team, supports team members and lets them "run with the ball." These organizations have the leadership and courage to stand back and let go," listen to the team and let them develop and work their plans for success.

Both the organization and the employees benefit by communicating the vision and strategy and by making it an open, trusting, supportive, and committed teaming environment.

Some of Patton's approaches would not fit in today's business environment and politically correct world. Patton's open use of profanity to get his point across would not play well today. His outspokenness and charged views on some sensitive topics would get him in more hot water than he ever experienced in the 1940s. Tolerance for nonconforming viewpoints on politically correct issues is low today and as a result the Patton of WWII would sadly be removed as a leader.

A BATTLE PLAN FOR LEADERSHIP

- Be tactically aggressive; Be a winner
- Have strength of character, trust, and integrity
- Have steadiness of purpose; Establish the plan and stay the course
- Accept responsibility and be accountable
- Show passion and commitment
- Lead from the front and be visible
- Keep it simple
- Be inspirational
- Establish the expectations and standards
- Leadership is not a popularity contest
- Communicate, communicate, communicate
- Set the example; Others will follow
- Be action oriented
- Do more than is required or expected; Go the extra mile
- Be decisive in your actions
- Be genuine and let people see the real, caring, and understanding you
- People don't necessarily need to like you, they need to respect you
- Leadership and management are not the same thing
- Treat others with respect; It goes both ways
- Provide the authority to match the responsibility
- Don't be a micromanager; Have faith and trust in your team
- Dress and act the part; Everyone is watching

CHAPTER 4
PATTON ON VISION AND STRATEGY

"A man must know his destiny... If he does not recognize it, then he is lost. By this I mean once, twice or at the most three times, fate will reach out and tap a man on the shoulder... If he has imagination, he will turn around and fate will point out to him what fork in the road he should take. If he has the guts, he will take it."

General George S. Patton

PATTON ON VISION

Patton believed in destiny and that his destiny was to become a great military leader. This was his vision and he started striving toward it at an early age. While a young boy, he told himself one day he would be a Lt General. Although he didn't really understand what that meant at the time, that was the long term vision he had for himself.

He always knew what he was to become, there was little doubt in his mind, and he let everyone around him know it as well. His vision was that he was born for one purpose and that purpose was to become a great military leader and hero: That was his destiny. Through careful study, planning, and training, he was able to attain that vision, or as he put it, his destiny. And in the last five or six years of his life he attained that vision and became one of the great military leaders of WWII.

He took great strides to ensure he looked and acted the part. This was true while he was at the Virginia Military Institute, at West Point, and throughout his career. A trait of Patton was that his uniform was impeccable and during his time at West Point, he would change it several times a day, just to maintain that smart military image. His manner of dress earned him the nickname "Gorgeous George."

In early 1935 Patton received orders to go back to Hawaii as the G-2 (Intelligence officer) for the General Staff Corps Hawaiian Department at Fort Shafter located outside Honolulu and Pearl Harbor.

While there, Patton observed and participated in several military maneuvers and at times was openly critical and blunt in his reports and feedback on the events. This negativity was primarily directed at the officers for their lack of imagination and poor leadership. He knew then how important it was that the training should be as realistic as possible and he didn't like what he was observing. It didn't meet his expectations and high standards. His vision was that leadership was a key and critical component to executing the strategy and to the success of an operation and he was not confident with the leadership being exhibited by those leading the exercise. The leaders were usually too far from the front and were focused more on their own comfort than the actual maneuver or exercise. They fell short of meeting his vision and expectations of leadership. During his time in Hawaii Patton was twice rated Superior, but there were also comments regarding his lack of tact in dealing with others. He worked on it, but even over time it never fully improved. Being outspoken and sometimes blunt was part of who he was.

Shortly after his arrival in Hawaii in 1935, and in true Patton fashion, he dug into naval warfare history. He studied the tactics, facts, high points, wins, losses, and lessons learned from over 300 years of naval invasions, which included those of Sir Francis Drake in the late 1580s right up through the events of World War I. His philosophy was to "Prepare for the unknown by studying how others in the past have coped with the unforeseeable and the unpredictable."

He took note of the successful elements of surprise, planning, night attacks, the needed cooperation between the ground and sea forces, and the intensity of the attack itself and above all, the need for strong leadership before, during, and after the battle. It was also during this time that he worked closely with the Navy, observing and participating in their operations and exercises. He was continually learning and gaining the knowledge that would help him attain his vision for himself and be successful during the upcoming events of WWII.

In June 1937 he wrote a paper titled "Surprise" and sent it the Chief of Staff at the Headquarters Hawaiian Department at Fort Shafter. In this paper Patton accurately predicted the events that took place on December 7, 1941 during the Japanese attack on Pearl Harbor. This was not a popular theory in 1937, but Patton believed that if a Japanese attack did occur, that it would come without warning, they would arrive in Hawaii off the normal sea lane traffic routes to a point 200 miles off Oahu, they would attack at night with carrier-based fighter and bomber aircraft, and that this attack would be preceded by the use of submarines. All of these actions were taken by the Japanese on December 7.

As part of that paper and vision, he laid out the elements of a strategy or plan for the defense of Pearl Harbor and the surrounding bases. He also developed a plan for the internment of the Japanese in Hawaii in the event of that surprise attack.

Through his study of history and the observations he had made regarding world events, Patton had the vision of a potential Japanese attack and had the courage to write a paper on his thoughts and send it up the chain of command.

His vision had struck gold earlier in his career. This vision was that technology should always be used to improve battle effectiveness. Very soon Patton was given an opportunity to do just that. He would use Dodge touring cars in Mexico in a publicized skirmish against Pancho Villa's troops.

On August 3, 1914, Germany declared war on France, thus beginning WWI. To fulfill his personal vision, Patton was eager to get into the fight and wrote a letter to General Wood, the Commanding General of the Eastern Department located at Governors Island, NY, asking for a one year leave to go to France at his own expense to "take part in this war." His request was denied, but he was still determined to get some battle experience.

In early 1915 Patton was notified that he would be receiving orders to the Philippines. This was not going to give Patton the battle experience he wanted, so in June he went to Washington, D.C. and "networked" to see if those orders could be changed. He was successful in that endeavor and received orders to Ft. Bliss Texas (El Paso) with the 8th Cavalry Regiment under General John "Blackjack" Pershing.

Pershing had recently been assigned to Ft. Bliss as part of a 4,800 troop military operation with the objective of capturing the infamous Mexican Revolutionary General Pancho Villa. This was termed the "Punitive Expedition" and ran from mid-March 1916 through early February 1917. At the time, Villa and his army were making raids against U.S. citizens in Texas and New Mexico and south of the border into northern Mexico. These attacks by Villa were the result of the decision made by the U.S. to support the current Mexican government, Villa's enemy, during the Mexican Revolution. Earlier in 1916, Villa's gang attacked Columbus, NM (roughly 75 miles west of El Paso and just over the U.S.-Mexico border), destroying the town and killing 18 people, including soldiers of the U.S. 13th Cavalry.

In the spring of 1916, Patton learned that his 8th Cavalry Regiment would not be part of the force pursuing Villa. Feeling left out again and with his need and desire for battle, just days before the forces' departure, Patton asked both the Regimental Adjutant and General Pershing's Adjutant to recommend that he become Pershing's aide. It was a gutsy and audacious move that paid off. He was given new orders the next day and two days later, Patton was en route to what would become the one of the first steps in the quest of his vision.

Accompanying the expedition were a series of trucks and aircraft, all of which were new technology and relatively new to the U.S. arsenal.

In mid-May 1916, Patton was sent out with 10 troops, two guides and three Dodge touring cars to obtain corn for the expedition's horses. While in the town of Rubio, Patton observed a group of 50-60 men that he deemed "a bad lot." Having spent the previous days vainly searching the nearby ranches and now sensing an opportunity to take prisoners—some possibly Villa's senior officers—Patton jumped at the chance and began to investigate. He laid out a plan for his troops and vehicles and conducted a search of the first ranch, but did not yield any results. However, at the second ranch, Patton and his men rode up in their touring cars with Patton in the lead and in no time found themselves in the midst of a shoot-out, which left three Mexican soldiers dead. Among the dead was one of General Villa's Colonels. Patton had the dead bodies tied to the hoods of the cars as trophies and returned to camp. This was the first time mechanized vehicles were used in battle by the U.S. Army. News of Patton's shoot-out made the press and Patton gained some national recognition. It is also said that Patton carved three notches in his pistol commemorating the event.

During WWI, he had a similar vision regarding new technology, and this one involved how the newly developed tank was going to be a major weapon of the U.S. arsenal and Patton wanted to be a part of it. In the fall of 1917, he wrote a letter to the Commander and Chief of the American Expeditionary Force (AEF) asking to be considered for a command of that service. In November 1917 Patton received orders and became the first officer of the AEF Tank Corps and went to Langres, France to establish the AEF tank school. After a short period of time, Patton was a tank expert and wrote a technical paper titled "Light Tanks," in which he highlighted and defined what a tank was, how the tank unit should be organized, and how it should be used in battle, or tactics. In later years Patton wrote across the top of his copy of that paper that "This paper was and is the Basis of the U.S. Tank Corps." Patton had a vision of the future importance of the tank and he was not only part of it, but he was establishing the vision and defining its use and strategy. He developed the tank and tank tactics as part of his vision and had a very strong commitment to it. He owned it and lived it.

In preparation for World War II, the U.S. felt the need for a desert training area similar to the areas of northern Africa and the Middle East. In the spring of 1942 Patton arrived in southern California and established the new Desert Training Center, which encompassed a huge 18,000 square mile area centered in Indio, CA, and included parts of Arizona and Nevada.

His vision was that he would be fighting the Germans in North Africa, so troops needed to be trained and ready for the harsh desert environment. Patton and his team developed and perfected the living and working conditions, tank tactics, methodologies and procedures at the Desert Training Center (DTC). The strategy was simply to "train like you fight" and the Desert Training Center was just the place, not only because of the physical living conditions, but also the realistic training operations and maneuvers that were conducted.

Patton's vision also extended to aviation. He obtained his pilot's license and saw aircraft as a valuable technological tool to be used in battle. That vision helped shape the training exercises at the DTC, as Patton used his airplane to get around the vast complex. He also had a radio installed in it so he could communicate with the ground. During maneuvers, he was often heard overhead providing guidance to the troops on the ground when things were not proceeding as he had planned.

He brought his taste for aircraft with him to North Africa and France during the war and was quickly able to see the front and keep close contact with his troops. Everyone knew that Patton was liable to pop up anywhere at any time and he used the aircraft to his advantage to support his vision and strategy.

Patton's Vision: To be a Great Military Leader. He saw it, wanted it, and pushed hard for it. He saw it and plotted his course to attain that vision, goal and objective. His leadership and involvement in the Battle of the Bulge drives this home.

From the June 6, 1944 D-Day landings to early December, the Allies were advancing well across Western Europe in their drive toward Berlin. However, the supply lines from Cherbourg, France were being stretched too thin. The port at Antwerp, Belgium was just opening up and supplies were just beginning to flow in, but it was yet to have a significant impact.

In December 1944 the Germans planned a major offensive in the Ardennes Forest area of France, Luxemburg, and Belgium. The focus and thrust of this offensive for the Germans was to drive west in a Blitzkrieg fashion, dividing the Allied forces north and south, splitting the Allied lines and retaking the port of Antwerp, thus cutting off the fledgling Allied supply route. At this time, the area of the Ardennes was used by the Allies as a reserve area that was poorly defended and was therefore the weak link. The Germans put this offensive together in secret with no radio traffic, moving men and equipment at night.

Once the Allies saw the offensive coming, it was too late: the Germans caught the Allies by surprise. The Germans began their offensive on December 16 across an 80-mile front. Eisenhower met with Patton and others on December 19 to determine the best course of action. To everyone's amazement, Patton audaciously committed to attack with two Divisions within 48 hours.

Patton was already heading east and would need to shift directions 90 degrees to head north and move his forces 100 miles to commence the attack. This was a huge undertaking especially considering the weather conditions of low clouds, poor visibility, and snow. What wasn't known was that Patton and his G-2 intelligence cadres had foreseen the offensive and were already preparing plans for the strategic shift. Shortly thereafter, the Germans surrounded the city of Bastogne and had the American 101st Airborne Division pinned down. Bastogne, Belgium served as a major transportation hub with 11 hard-topped roads funneling into it. It was of critical strategic importance to both the Germans and Allies during the Battle of the Bulge and became the center piece of the battle.

Patton once said "make your plans fit the circumstances." It was truly fitting for the circumstances he faced. Patton, in true fashion, shifted his direction 90 degrees north (a very complicated and complex maneuver) and drove troops and himself hard through very difficult conditions and terrible weather. He was determined to free the 101st by Christmas. It was at this time that Patton asked Colonel James O' Neill, the 3rd Army Chaplain, to write a prayer asking for good weather. The prayer was as follows:

> *Almighty and merciful Father, we humbly beseech thee, of thy great goodness, to restrain these immoderate rains with which we have had to contend. Grant us fair weather for battle. Graciously hearken to us soldiers who call upon thee that, armed with thy power, we may advance from victory to victory and crush the oppression and wickedness of our enemies, and establish thy justice among men and nations.*
> *Amen.*

On the morning of December 23, the weather cleared (Patton later awarded Col. O'Neill a Bronze Star for his efforts) and he attacked the German forces at Bastogne, rescuing the 101st on December 26. He had a vision of what he wanted to accomplish, committed himself and his troops to that vision, and then developed and executed a strategy, including prayer, to make it successful.

VISION IN BUSINESS

After leadership, the next most important fundamental building block of any successful organization is the development of the organizational vision. This is where it all starts and it sets the stage for the next steps in building the organizational foundation.

This organizational vision is what defines and highlights what I like to say is "Who or what we want to be when we grow up." Who do we want to become? When I was growing up I wanted to fly military fighter aircraft. That was my vision at the time. It is what I wanted to do and become. At a young age, Patton's vision was to be a great military leader and to lead a large army in combat. It set the stage and his motivation for what he was to become.

In most chaotic organizations, if there is a vision or a plan, it is usually loose, not well documented, or communicated and as a result, not fully understood by the workforce. These plans are often found sitting on a shelf in the president's office collecting dust, where they will most likely sit until pulled out late next year in preparation for the next year's budget, and that's a maybe. The bottom line is that from an organizational perspective, there is no plan and as such you cannot move the chaotic organization forward.

I find that for many businesses today, leadership has not developed a true vision for the organization or if it has, it's vague and has not been fully communicated or explained so that everyone sees, feels, and understands it. As a result, it is unclear to the organization where it is going and why it wants to go there. Without a vision, folks do not understand or know which direction you as the leader want to take. They are lost.

A vision for an organization defines where it is going and depicts a future state of the organization and "what it is going to be like when we get there." Or what it will become. In order to attain that vision, it's critical that it is well communicated and fully understood by all that are involved.

A vision defines why the organization exists and helps in establishing pride in everyone's involvement with that organization. It's our image and helps define who we want to become or our future state. It establishes pride in us as part of that organization. It clarifies who we are and where we are going and assists in gaining the necessary participants to buy in to what we want to become. As I mentioned in the Introduction, back in the 1950s and 1960s the vision for America was clear. We knew who we were, where were going, and how we were going to get there, and we were proud of ourselves and our accomplishments. We've lost that feeling today. Today that vision is not clear. It's cloudy and out of focus.

The vision is critical in defining who and what we want to become, where we are going, and without it, we are a nothing but a wandering generality. For an organization to be successful, it must be able to see, feel, smell, taste, and understand the vision if they are going to be part of it.

Key phrases for vision:

- Defines who/what we want to be when we grow up
- Highlights what it will be like when we get there
- Explains why we want to go there
- See it, Feel it, Smell it, Taste it. Be it!

Without the vision, or sense of where you are headed, your future comments will often start with "I wish I/we would have done this…" Without a vision, you can't plot a direction or a strategy (plan) as to how you are going to get there. It's the second step in *Moving Forward* or *Accelerating Performance*.

STRATEGY

Patton once said to "use a steamroller strategy, that is make up your mind on a course and direction and stick to it!" He also said that "Strategy and tactics do not change; only the means of applying them is different." Both statements were true when he wrote them and they still hold true in today's business.

The word "strategy" actually comes from a military context and refers to an action plan that is developed to achieve a specific goal or objective. It lays out the path as to how we are going to get there.

To be meaningful and ensure success, the strategy needs to be specific in nature and detailed in its preparation. It has to be very clear and well communicated. This is just as true in business as it is in battle. Strategy is the third building block in the foundation of getting the organization on the same page and plots the course, actions, and steps as to how it is going to get to the destination or vision. It is The Plan. It deems which actions are important, in what order, and according to what timeline. To put it simply, the strategy details what everyone needs to perform in order to attain the vision. It helps clarify how everyone operates and operates together. It clarifies and defines how everything they do supports the vision.

PATTON ON STRATEGY

As for Patton, at an early age he knew who and what he wanted to become and he plotted his course as to how he was going to get there. He had his strategy right down to the war face he practiced in the mirror. His time at West Point and every assignment he held afterward was in support of his personal strategy to attain his vision. On a personal level, he knew where he wanted to go and plotted the path and strategy as to how he was going to get there.

As part of that strategy, Patton studied and conducted his own research on Gen. Pershing, Napoleon, Fredrick the Great, and other military leaders to understand their strengths so he could emulate them, thus making himself a better leader and bringing him closer to his vision. He would routinely type out inspiring quotes from these leaders and use them for his motivation. His personal vision was to be a great military leader and as part of his strategy to accomplish his vision, he studied and learned from what he felt were great military leaders both past and present. He learned from their accomplishments and victories in battle and he strived to emulate their traits and characteristics.

As part of his strategy, he studied military history and used what he learned in developing his own thoughts about warfare, potential strategies, and tactics. His studies included anything war related that he could get his hands on. Despite his feelings for the Germans, he read many of the WWI German accounts.

Frederick the Great and Napoleon were both heavy readers. Patton learned from this and was himself very well read, especially on military history. During his trip to North Africa and in preparation for Operation Torch, Patton read the Koran so he could gain a better understanding of the Moroccan people.

Like Frederick the Great, Patton did not believe in digging in and taking the defensive: He was always on the offense. One quote personifies this mentality most: *"Go Forward! Always Go Forward!"*

Frederick and Napoleon believed that a leader should lead from the front. Pershing also spent considerable time visiting his troops on the front lines during WWI and Patton did the same, emulating those great leaders and insisting that his officers do so as well.

Patton, Napoleon, and Frederick took exceptional care of their troops' needs. All three were strong believers in letting advanced artillery (technology) do most of the work to spare the lives of troops. This was part of their strategy.

Patton learned from and copied the fearless persona displayed by Pershing, Frederick, and Napoleon of exhibiting calmness during battle. Again, all this was part of his personal and professional strategy.

All three of these historical leaders possessed an inherent ability for strategy and planning. Patton did as well.

Patton was very involved in the strategic planning aspects of "Operation Torch," a joint Allied invasion of North Africa in November 1942 just 11 months after the U.S. entered the war. Patton was in command of the Western Task Force, and 24,000 troops that would come ashore near Casablanca. He divided his force into thirds and put in place what he felt were strong leaders over each. Going into battle Patton was confident in his strategy, but apprehensive as well.

With the joint naval operations experience he had picked up during his tours in Hawaii, Patton was well-schooled in these types of amphibious landings. He provided his thoughts and guidance and his input was accepted. Patton had learned and understood the importance of coordination between the Navy and Army and as such spent considerable time with the Navy in the development of the Torch Strategy. He was intimately involved in the entire battle plan before the troops hit the beach and was extremely hands on once they were ashore.

"A competent leader can get efficient service from poor troops, while on the contrary an incapable leader can demoralize the best of troops," General Pershing once said. Patton thought along the same lines. The success of a military operation rested with the leadership.

These great leaders preceding Patton all had the innate ability to make sound decisions during battle. Patton followed suit by training himself and his troops constantly so that decisions came naturally during actual combat.

STRATEGY IN BUSINESS

Once you've fully defined and communicated the vision, the next fundamental building block to running a successful business is the development of the strategy. It establishes the business plan, direction, actions, execution sequence, and time lines for the business as you *Go Forward* to attain the vision. I am amazed at how many businesses operate today without a real, defined, and documented strategy. They could be so much further ahead if they just had a plan. A strategy helps keep the business on track. Without it the organization will lose direction, get off course, and lose momentum.

In many businesses, there often isn't a strategy or, if there is one, it's superficial, vague, and cloudy. Like the vision, if the strategy is not clear and understood by all those involved, then it's not clear what the organization needs to do. Without a strategy, the organization is in effect working in the dark, not knowing if what they are doing is correct or in support of the vision. The strategy is the path or roadmap used by a business as it *Moves Forward* to meet or fulfill the vision. Leaders need to lead the organization in the development of the strategy.

"Good tactics can save even the worst Strategy. Bad tactics will destroy even the best Strategy." This is just as true in business as it is in the military. Work with your team and lead them in the development of the strategy and underlying departmental actions or tactics. "Don't tell people how to do things, tell them what to do and let them surprise you with their results." Listen and let them develop the plan as to how to get there.

As an example, I've worked with several organizations that lacked clear and definitive strategies. I'd ask the employees what they thought the strategy was and their response was simply to make the sales figures or shipments for the month no matter what they needed to do. As a result, as they reached for monthly shipments or large sales dollars, they had several problems. On time delivery was poor yet inventory was high. They would ship the higher valued sales orders early and let the less expensive orders sit because they took more work and were not needed to meet the directed sales volume. They were also shipping more than 80% of their monthly shipments in the last three days of the month, resulting in very poor quality and high overtime the last 10 days of the month.

This was caused by not establishing an honest production flow and only working on what needed to ship for the month in order to make the sales quota. At the beginning of the month there was nothing close to completion so the push was to get as much done by month end as possible. As problems manifested themselves and the organization ran out of time, the month-end push would drive overtime and lower quality standards.

Why was it like this? It was because the workforce did not know or understand what was really important. Their drive and motivation were focused strictly on making the monthly shipping or sales quota because that's what the folks upstairs wanted. The importance wasn't on the how they made the numbers, but on the numbers themselves. The organization typically functioned in a short sighted crisis mode where constantly changing priorities and chaos were the norm. The ancillary negative results were an outcome of the indirect strategy of "Making the Month" in regard to the projected sales figures.

To be clear, if an organization does not have a strategy then it is not clear what needs to be done and the business lacks direction. This causes confusion, frustration, and organizational misalignment as the company lacks an overall understanding of what's truly important. Without a clear direction, plan, or roadmap, departments will set their own course to achieve what they think the folks upstairs want.

The strategic process starts with an overall business strategy which generally includes:

- Business Vision or Objective
- Organizational Objectives
- Comprehensive Market and Competitive Analysis
- Departmental Action Plans
- Resource Needs and Requirements to Implement the Action Plans
- Values and Expectations for When and How These Are to Be Attained

Simply put, once the leadership and vision for the business are established, a high level overall business strategy is then compiled followed by individualized departmental strategies. These departmental strategies (or plans) support and drive the overall strategy. Once this process is complete it is then possible to develop underlying and specific departmental/individual tactics or actions to further support the strategy. Everything flows into the plan to meet and fulfill the vision.

I too often see organizations implementing actions (tactics) with no understanding of the strategy. These actions for the sake of action are often unfocused and result in more confusion and organizational frustration as departmental and/or personal tactics or actions conflict. Without a clear strategy, there cannot be a platform or foundation on which to *Move Forward*.

CONCLUSION - VISION & STRATEGY

Again, to be successful in both the military and business environments, you must have a strategy in order to attain the vision. Having a strategy is just as critical in business as it is in battle. You must have a plan if you are going to win. The analogy is:

- A Lack of Strategy in the Military = Unnecessary Fatalities, Battle Damage, Lost Resources, and Lost Battles

- Business – Strategy = Limited Growth, Inefficiencies, Higher Costs, Confusion, Frustration, Low Morale, High Employee Turnover, and Unsatisfied Customers

Things don't just "happen." In order to get to where we want to go, we need a plan.

As an illustration, I want to drive from Dallas, TX to San Diego, CA. I don't just get in my car and drive, do I? I need to know how I am going to get there. There are things that need to be understood and checked before I just get in the car and drive. These include items such as the condition of the car, oil, fluid levels, tires, route, road conditions, fuel stops, weather, timing, motels, clothes to take, maps, GPS, cell phone, money, food, lodging… There is a lot to consider in my trip plan or strategy before I start heading west. The vision is getting to San Diego and the strategy is all the items listed above.

Patton said it best: "It is funny how easy it is to do things once one has a plan to do." A business strategy is just that: A plan or roadmap of things to do in order to attain your vision.

Patton always had a plan, both in his personal life and military career; he always knew where he was going and how he was going to get there.

I've been the same way in my life. I had dreams and aspirations (a vision) of being a military fighter pilot and later a senior executive and business leader. And early in my career I developed my strategy and plan: Education first, then the military, sales, business development, operations, mid-senior level leadership, and then multiple business turnaround experiences. In addition and as part of my plan, I've operated in multiple aerospace markets—aircraft, turbine engines, aircraft structures, machining, assembly, electromechanical, instruments and avionics in both the original equipment manufacturing (OEM) and maintenance repair and overhaul (MRO) segments. These were all part of my strategy to end up with a well rounded background in order to fulfill my vision of running my own company. Today I am the Founder and CEO of *The Tomcat Group*, focused on assisting business leaders in *Accelerating Business Performance* in their organizations. My strategy worked.

In the businesses I have run, like Patton, I've always had a vision and strategy. I felt it was one of the critical elements of leadership to establish the vision and plot the strategic course for the organization, setting out how we were going to get there. That strategy was detailed, well communicated, and understood by the workforce and was fundamental in the growth and development of the business.

The development and communication of the vision and strategy were key factors for General Patton and played a major role in the success of the operational and financial turnarounds I have conducted. I am convinced that without a vision and strategy, those turnarounds would not have been successful.

A Battle Plan for Vision and Strategy

Vision

- To be successful, an organization needs to know where it is going (vision)
  - o The vision establishes where do you want to go and why you want to go there
- Once established, the vision needs to be actively communicated
- As a leader you need to highlight what it will be like when we attain the vision

- Be able to see it, feel it, smell it, taste it. Be it!

- Without knowing where you are going (vision) you cannot develop a plan to get there

STRATEGY

- To be successful, you have to have a plan.

- The plan or roadmap details how you are going to attain the vision.

- Patton: "Make your plans fit the circumstances."

- This plan or strategy must be well defined, clear, concise, and comprehensive.

- Work with and lead your team in developing the strategy.

- The strategy must be openly and continually communicated and understood at all levels of the organization.

- The strategy defines what is important and the organization strives to attain the vision.

- Implementing actions without a strategy will not yield lasting results.

- As a leader you must be committed to the strategy and have the courage to stay the course.

- The strategy should contain the following elements:

  o Organizational Objectives

  o Comprehensive Market and Competitive Analysis

  o Departmental Action Plans

  o Resource Requirements to Implement the Action Plans

  o Values and Expectations for What, When, and How It Is to Be Attained

  o The strategy should be routinely reviewed; If needed you will Adjust, Adapt and Overcome.

- Study other leaders and learn from their success and accomplishments.

- Patton: "Strategy and tactics do not change, only the means of applying them is different."

- Patton: "Good tactics can save even the worst Strategy. Bad tactics will destroy even the best Strategy."

CHAPTER 5
PATTON ON THE THREE A'S
AND PERFORMANCE METRICS

*"Strategy and tactics do not change;
only the means of applying them is different."*

General George S. Patton

Now that the leadership, vision, and strategy building blocks have been established, we next focus on the basic structural elements of execution: The Three A's.

Back in elementary school we were taught the Three R's:

- **R**eading
- w**R**iting
- a**R**ithmetic

(I know, I am dating myself!!!)

For today's business environment, the Three R's get a new twist and become The Business Three A's:

- **A**lignment
- **A**ction
- **A**ccountability

These fundamental building blocks are the critical components listed on the Six Elements of Business Success pyramid:

Six Elements of Business Success

PATTON AND THE THREE A'S

Patton disliked chaos and disorder, and as a result his personality made a great fit for the military. It provided him with the structure and means by which to operate and provided him an opportunity to function, perform, and excel. A prime example of this is that Patton always aligned his actions and held himself and others accountable. He believed and functioned under a distinct and sometimes rigid order of things, processes, and procedures. He believed in hierarchy and followed the Chain of Command.

As discussed earlier, when Patton took over II Corps after the U.S. disaster at Kasserine Pass in the African theater during WWII, there had been a lack of leadership and discipline. There was weak plan or strategy, no alignment and no actions and as a result, no one was truly held accountable. Patton started making changes immediately and instilled from the very beginning the equivalent of what I call The Three A's. He did this in a direct, no-nonsense manner and supplied the needed accountability.

He very quickly set expectations for performance, direction, and discipline by instituting fines for uniform violations. This highlighted what Patton deemed important and instilled order and direction within the organization. He made it clear to everyone what he wanted and expected. He got the organization aligned, heading in the right direction and he did it subconsciously by using The Three A's.

Several months later this concept proved successful during the battle of El Guettar where he defeated the German troops. The discipline, order, expectations, and training paid off.

Patton effectively used these principles as well during his time with the 7th Army in Sicily as he pushed to Palermo and then on to Messina and also during his time with the 3rd Army in Europe.

In Sicily, Patton's 7th Army's role was secondary as he was to support and protect British General Montgomery's western flank as the Brits pushed north towards Messina. However, Patton was determined to demonstrate the combat effectiveness of the American soldier and as a result was unsatisfied with a potentially inglorious support role. Instead, he devised a strategy to have his forces first push west and then northwest to Palermo and then press east along the coast to Messina. His vision was to get to Messina before Montgomery and he developed a strategy to pull it off.

In accordance with The Three A's, with his strategy developed, he aligned his forces to continue the support of Montgomery, but also developed a coordinated and deliberate action plan and aligned other forces to move westward down the south coast and take the port city of Agrigento. These efforts and actions were approved by General Alexander, but Patton's ultimate plan was to then head north to Palermo, and he developed his next set of actions to accomplish just that. He wanted the recognition for both himself and his 7th Army proving the combat capability of the American soldier. Once Palermo was taken and he took possession of two roads to Messina, Patton was on his way east with the purpose of arriving in Messina before Montgomery. He successfully accomplished that objective and earned the recognition he so desired.

He was also working the accountability aspect during these events in leading his troops to advance at an accelerated pace. He was always in his vehicle up at the front making sure things were *Going Forward*. He led and drove not only the alignment and action side, but was also a key factor in the accountability as well.

Patton had a vision and a strategy for getting to Messina before British General Montgomery and through an informal Three A's process developed the alignment, actions and accountability to execute that strategy successfully and attain the vision.

THE BUSINESS THREE A's DEFINED

Over the years, I've had the opportunity to work with quite a few business organizations. Some were very well run businesses where everything just seemed to flow and come together. Others were operating in a state of chaos where everything seemed to be in a constant state of confusion, resulting in high stress, high cost, low productivity, low employee morale, and low levels of customer satisfaction. "A soldier must know his objective and what he is doing at all times," meaning if he doesn't, then you have the poorly run business scenario described above, but in a military setting.

Once the vision and strategy have been developed, The Three A's work in unison and harmony as these three elements support each other in the execution of the strategy. Let's begin by talking about each element independently.

ALIGNMENT

As we discussed in the previous chapter, I have found that the first fundamental building blocks of any successful business are the organization's leadership, vision, and strategy. Without these critical elements, the business has no direction, is operating without a captain or rudder, and becomes a wandering generality.

In looking at the dichotomy between these two types of organizations, I find the primary difference between a well run business and one that struggles is the alignment provided by that clear leadership, vision and strategic plan.

The lack of a vision and strategic plan drives organizational confusion and misalignment as the organization heads off into unguided and, too often, unintended directions. In several organizations, I have asked the workforce for their interpretation of the company's strategic plan and in most cases the answer was simply "Make the Month" or as I call it, "MTM," making the projected sales for the month. Without a vision or plan, this becomes the default objective because that is what they constantly hear from the folks upstairs. So MTM becomes the primary focus of the organization and the organization aligns itself in that manner. It's a natural cause and effect scenario. As we discussed earlier, this MTM mentality drives the organization in the wrong direction causing month-end shipment "hockey sticks" where most of the monthly sales are shipped at the end of the month, increased inventory, poor on-time delivery, reduced customer satisfaction, reduced cash flow, low employee morale, and stress and chaos within the organization.

The vision and strategic Plan are the answer to the question: "Who do we want to be when we grow up?" They define where we want to go. They are the key to setting the organization's direction. Alignment is the first step in keeping our efforts focused on executing the strategy as we *Move Forward*.

This alignment is accomplished by breaking the strategy down into small, specific sets and subsets of objectives that support each other and feed the execution of the strategy.

The first step is establishing three to five clearly defined overall organizational objectives. These first tier organizational objectives serve to support the overall strategy, and set the stage for the next tier of organizational objectives as they are rolled out across departments. In turn, each area (or department) then supplies its own three to five supporting objectives specific to its department, which in turn provide the basis for the next tier's objectives and the next and the next. This objective setting process continues to the lowest level of the organization. Each tier's objectives support and feed into the next levels. Think of it as "bubbling up" or building a pyramid as they flow together. An example of an objective hierarchy is given below.

GOAL AND OBJECTIVE HIERARCHY

With the establishment of the leadership, vision, strategic plan, and supporting organizational, departmental, and lower level interdepartmental objectives, you now have the foundation for true organizational alignment. Again, this alignment is what sets the organization's priorities and defines what should be important for each area and department in order to support and execute the strategy. It is what gets different departments on the same page and going in the same direction.

ACTION

Once the alignment elements are established, it will then be necessary to develop specific and detailed action plans for each objective put together as part of the alignment process. Here is where the specific action steps (or tactics) are compiled that will lead in accomplishing each objective supporting the strategy. Actions define what we specifically need to do in order to meet the objective and are put together in a predetermined order or sequence. Each action should be a clear and definitive set of steps that lead the way to meeting the objective. Think of the actions as a detailed mini-strategy. It's the roadmap and sequence of steps that need to be undertaken to meet the objective.

As an example, if one of the objectives were to reduce the amount of scrap generated during the manufacturing process, then we would expect to see a definitive list of the actions specifically designed and focused toward meeting that objective. We will discuss action plans later in this chapter.

As these actions are accomplished in sequence, the organization begins to *Move Forward* and proceeds with executing the strategy and taking steps towards attaining the vision.

ACCOUNTABILITY

Now that the alignment and actions have been established, we need to talk about the third Business A's: Accountability.

Accountability is a basic concept that sometimes gets lost in the shuffle. As we discussed earlier, it starts with getting to work on time, getting to meetings on time, being prepared for the meetings, and completing tasks or actions on time. Basically, employees need to be held accountable for their job performance. We sometimes lose this concept as we struggle to hold employees accountable in our "don't upset anyone" or "I might get sued" politically correct environments. You don't have to be a tyrant, but have the leadership abilities to set the standards and expectations and the courage to follow through with the consequences.

Often times what is missing in these scenarios is the setting of the leaders' expectations and resulting consequences of not performing up to or meeting those expectations. If an individual is not aware of the expectations, or does not understand the consequences for falling short of those expectations, and we as leaders fail to follow through on the consequences, then the organization fails to *Move Forward*. It remains at a standstill. We can develop the best strategy and actions, but if we fail to follow through on execution, then the organization fails to *Move Forward*.

As part of the accountability segment, with the development of the organizational and departmental objectives, it is possible to develop a specific set of objectives or actions for individuals that feed and support the department objectives, which drive the organizational objectives.

These three to five employee objectives would then be built into an incentive compensation plan that would financially reward the employee for his or her performance. This performance reward program will reinforce and assist in keeping the needed organizational alignment within the organization and drive accountability. I recommend that these objectives be reviewed with the employee at least quarterly in order to track performance, provide the employee with feedback, and adjust the actions as necessary to ensure meeting the objectives that feed the strategy.

By establishing individual employee goals and objectives, you are also reinforcing the organizational alignment process by aligning the individual's actions to the strategy. This is accomplished because once these individual employee goals and objectives are established, you now have the employee goals aligned with the departmental goals, which are aligned with the overall organizational goals. They all feed and support each other and are key elements in the execution of the strategy.

The employees also need to understand that they will be held responsible and accountable for their performance. They will be held accountable for their actions in relation to those objectives and the results of those actions. The employee's annual performance evaluation and the employee's financial reward are fundamental to the accountability element. With a thorough understanding of their objectives, the setting of expectations, and access to the necessary resources, they are in a position to take ownership and follow them through to completion. They are in control of the outcome.

If we are to have an organization *Move Forward*, not only is it important to get everyone on the same page with objectives and actions, but people must be held accountable for the execution and follow through on those action items. If people are not held accountable for their performance, then the actions will not meet the objectives and successfully execute the strategy.

As noted in the Six Elements of Business Success diagram, Accountability is at the top of the pyramid just under Success. In order to hold individuals accountable, we need to have the first five building blocks in place.

Without the individual accountability for completion of the actions, the organization will not be in a position to *Move Forward* and will remain stagnant. This basic and fundamental concept is critical to the execution of the strategy and is often overlooked in our politically correct environments.

The supporting elements of accountability are the first five elements of a successful business with Accountability at the top just under Success. We need to have the first five, before we can have accountability. To help in leading accountability, we as leaders need to set the expectations, the consequences, and the follow-through.

To help foster the accountability, this element is made up of three to five clearly defined employee performance objectives that "bubble up" into the departmental and organizational objectives. For this to be successful, the employee must have the tools, training, and experience to take full ownership of accomplishing the objectives and reaping the rewards.

PERFORMANCE METRICS

With the establishment of the Business Three A's, we can now develop and implement a series of organizational performance metrics that will track our progress as we strive for business success.

For keeping score in business, the initial performance metrics are the company's financial statements. It's not unlike the military, which tracks miles traveled, towns liberated, gallons of gasoline used, ammo used, number killed, number wounded, number captured… It's a little different, but understanding the financials and how they were put together is crucial in order to be successful in business.

In running a business it is important that you understand what makes up, feeds, or drives those financials and it's crucial that you understand how they all interrelate. We need to have full understanding as to how they arrived at those numbers and what path the organization took to get there. During some operation reviews I've attended, senior management will immediately jump directly to the bottom line or cash and begin banging away and demanding better performance, many times without understanding what is behind those numbers.

We need to keep in mind that if you are going to improve or *Accelerate the Performance* of any organization, you cannot begin to affect that performance until you have a full understanding of the financials, what makes them up, and how they interrelate. We need to understand that if I make a change or adjustment in one area, it will have an effect in another area.

I like to use the analogy of flying an airplane when speaking of financial statements. When flying an airplane on instruments you must pay attention to all the gauges in the cockpit. You have to constantly scan your altitude, airspeed, heading, climb rate, engine instruments, and fuel gauge. You also need to understand that if you try to climb without adding power to the engine, the airspeed will drop. And that if you turn, there will be a need to add power and raise the nose to compensate for the loss of lift during that turn. Financial statements operate in a similar fashion and we need to understand those cause and effect relationships.

I've worked with several organizations where the senior leader spent very little time with the finance folks while they worked through the month, quarter, or yearend financials. All the leader would ask is "How'd we do?" and leave it to the finance leader to sort it out. Again, you cannot effectively lead a business and have it *Move Forward* and *Accelerate Performance* if you do not understand and have the ability to explain the financials.

I've seen some organizations where the financials are not understood by anyone outside the finance department. Many staff members do not understand rather simple calculations such as cash flow, inventory turns, absorption, purchase price variance, or accruals. As such, it is difficult to get the staff to understand (or align) how their actions, or inactions, have an impact on the financials. As business leaders, it is important to take the time and get your staff, and potentially the next level down, to have a solid understanding of the financial statements for your business, what makes them up, and how they interrelate. If everyone understands this, then the organizational alignment and accountability will be much easier to attain. By getting everyone educated and up to speed on what makes up the financials, how they are calculated, and how they interact and flow, you'll get everyone on the same page and speaking the same language. "We can never get anything across unless we talk the language of the people we are trying to instruct." If the staff doesn't understand the financials, then you can't talk to them about the numbers.

When reviewing a set of financials, it's difficult to perform any analysis without looking at trends. If inventory turns suddenly increases from 2 to 12, then there has to be a reason. It didn't happen by magic. By reviewing trends, we get a better understanding of what is taking place beyond the numbers. By analyzing trends, you can view a movie rather than a snapshot of the organization's performance.

In analyzing the numbers, it's not only important to understand them, but also to get beyond the numbers themselves. If one month gross margins slip and the bottom line improves, you'll need to dig into why. Were there improvements in other areas of the financials that made up for the poor gross margins? Regardless of the bottom line performance, it is important to dig into the gross margin slippage and fully understand what makes it up and why it happened. Once that's understood, you're in a position to remedy the issue instead of letting it fester or hoping it fixes itself. Remember, hope is not a strategy.

When only looking at the financials without a full understanding of what is driving the numbers or how they interrelate, things break down. For instance, management implements a No Overtime policy and the following month, shipments are down. These low shipments could be because that overtime was needed to counteract the production inefficiencies in the manufacturing area, the extra time was needed because supplier parts were late, or the organization didn't have enough direct labor resources to support the production flow. To be effective, we need to understand cause and effect relationships. It is critical that business leaders understand the whole picture and not just a snapshot of the financials. We need to understand what's behind those financials before taking action.

It all interrelates. It's a big dynamic 10,000 piece puzzle with lots of moving pieces. We need to understand how they all interrelate so we can understand the Action - Reaction effects.

Patton looked at the entire battle and understood the big picture. He knew that a true understanding of that big picture included the ground action, air cover, supplies, ammo, fuel, replacements, lines on communication, and more. He was on top of all of it and based on his experience and the information available, he was able to make the needed changes and decisions necessary to ensure success in battle.

In business we need to see the entire picture, understand the drivers and the inter-relationships and then, as Patton did, develop and implement our actions, or tactics, to remedy and make our business successful.

Once the vision, strategy, alignment, actions and accountability are established, this becomes the driving force behind the creation of a supportive set of performance metrics beyond the financials. These performance metrics assist in maintaining alignment by tracking what's important, but also provide feedback as we track how effective our actions are in regards to meeting/improving the metric or objective, thus reinforcing metrics are an integral part of the alignment, action and accountability process and will provide performance feedback as to how your plan is meeting the objective or strategy. To put it simply, the performance metrics supplement the financials and track your progress in the execution of the strategy. It's a feedback loop. Remember the old adage, that what gets measured gets done.

THE BALANCED SCORECARD (BSC)

I've had great success with a performance metrics system called the Balanced Scorecard or BSC. The BSC format is a simple, one page system that is segmented into four distinct functional areas:

1. Financial: These are the standard business financial statements right out of the system. It's nothing fancy, just the normal financials.

2. Customer: These are a series of metrics as viewed directly by the customer. This may include on-time delivery, orders past due, warranty returns, customer quality measurements, new orders…anything that may be viewed as critical from the customer's perspective.

3. Internal Processes: These are metrics from within our organization that we feel impact our ability to meet customer and financial expectations. This may include product margins, supplier on-time delivery, labor and material variances, overtime, interdepartmental on-time delivery, engineering changes, WIP (Work in Process), scrap, rework, open employee requisitions, safety, labor utilization, equipment availability, or anything that could positively or adversely affect our customer and financial goals and objectives.

4. Investment: These are areas where we opt to make investments to drive our internal processes, to meet the customer requirements in order to meet our overall financial objectives. This may include capital expenditures, training, outside consulting, R&D activities, or any other investment to keep the organization moving forward.

In preparation of the BSC, each area of the scorecard will have three to 10 areas of measurement that highlight the organization's performance. In turn, these metrics track and report the organization's actual performance against specific targets, thus highlighting the progress of the strategy.

Each metric is posted and compared to the forecast and budget. Each metric is then colored coded green, yellow or red just like a traffic stoplight, based on its performance to what has been forecast.

- Any metric that is better than forecast is coded green.

- Any metric underperforming within 5% of forecast is coded yellow.

- Any metric that is underperforming by more than 5% of forecast is coded red.

Think of the Balanced Scorecard as an engine in which investment feeds the internal processes and turns them green, which feed the customer metrics turning them green, which the drive the financials and turn them green. If the financials are not green then we drop down to the investment section and work ourselves back up the BSC looking for areas that need improvement to drive the rest of the metrics green.

These metrics work together and the format provides a single page, clear and uncluttered picture of the organizational performance.

An example of a Balanced Scorecard is given below.

ABC Company
Balanced Scorecard
December 2010

Area	Measurement	Owner	Month Actual	Forecast	Var Fsct	Budget
FINANCE	Sales (x1000)	MF	$ 2,423	$ 2,715	$ (292)	$ 2,715
	Gross Profit AOC(x1000)	MF	$ (245)	$ 495	$ (740)	$ 495
	MG&A (x1000)	MF	$ 250	$ 340	$ 90	$ 340
	EBITDA (x1000)	MF	$ (960)	$ 170	$ (1,130)	$ 170
	Cash (x1000)	MF	$ 234	$ 133	$ 101	$ 133
	Orders (x1000)	MF	$ 3,517	$ 2,923	$ 594	$ 2,923
	Inventory (x1000)	MF	$ 9,475	$ 10,110	$ (635)	$ 10,110
	Inventory Turns	MF	1.23	1.62	-0.39	1.62
	Sales/Employee	MF	$ 25.24	$ 28.28	$ (3)	$ 28.28
CUSTOMER	On-Time-Delivery %	PM	58%	52%	6%	
	SO Lines Delivered On-Time	PM	11	12	-1	
	SO Line Items Delivered Late	PM	8	11	-3	
	WIP Line Items Past Due (#)	PM	18	10	8	
	WIP Line Items Past Due (%)	PM	11%	9%	2%	
	Warranty Returns (#)	RD	14	5	9	
	Warranty Costs (x1000)	LG	$50	$50	$ (1)	
	Warranty No Fault Found (#)	RD	0	1	-1	
	Warranty No Fault Found ($)	RD	$0	$750	$ (750)	
Internal	Overtime (DL) %	MF	5.3%	5.00%	0.3%	
	Kit OTD%	CD			0%	
	Supplier OTD (%)	CD	34%	92%	-58%	
	Open Purchase Orders	CD	416	625	-209	
	Past Due Purchase Orders	CD	27	50	-23	
	SCAR's Open	JS	2	4	2	
	SCAR's Issued	JS	2	4	2	
	SCAR's Closed	JS	4	3	1	
	SCAR's Past Due	JS	0	2	-2	
	Scrap ($)	MF	$11,400	$5,000	$6,400	
	NCR's Written	JS	32	42	-10	
	Squawks Written	JS	41	80	-39	
	Rework	MF	$3,400	$3,000	$400	
	ERO's Released	LO	36	35	1	
	ERO/ECO's Initiated	LO	112	180	-68	
	ECO's Released	LO	26	65	-39	
	Redlines Off the Floor	LO	15	45	-30	
	Total FT Employees	LM	85	86	-1	
	Direct/Indirect Ratio	MF	61%	60%	1%	
	Total Temps/PT/Contr.	LM	8	8	0	
	Open Employment Reqs	LM	6	7	-1	
	Internal Audits Conducted	JS	0	0	0	
	External Audits Conducted	JS	0	0	0	
	CAR's Open	JS	4	4	0	
	CAR's Issued	JS	0	3	-3	
	CAR's Closed	JS	3	3	0	
	CAR's Past Due	JS	0	1	-1	
	Cost of Quality	MF	$64,300	$58,000	$6,300	
	Housekeeping	CG	85%	95%	-10%	
	Safety	CG	90%	95%	-5%	
Invest	Training Hours	LM	35.66	45	-9.34	
	CAPEX	MF	$7,000	$50,000	$ 43,000	
	R&D	MF	$0	$25,000	-$25,000	

ABC Company (Continued)
Balanced Scorecard
December 2010

Area	Measurement	Owner	Year to Date			
			Actual	Forecast	Var Fsct	Budget
FINANCE	Sales (x1000)	MF	$ 5,426	$ 6,559	$ (1,133)	$ 6,559
	Gross Profit AOC(x1000)	MF	$ 720	$ 1,259	$ (539)	$ 1,259
	MG&A (x1000)	MF	$ 690	$ 840	$ 150	$ 840
	EBITDA (x1000)	MF	$ (412)	$ 465	$ (877)	$ 465
	Cash (x1000)	MF	$ 1,632	$ 431	$ 1,201	$ 431
	Orders (x1000)	MF	$ 3,821	$ 8,378	$ (4,557)	$ 8,378
	Inventory (x1000)	MF				
	Inventory Turns	MF				
	Sales/Employee	MF	$ 18.97	$ 22.93	$ (4)	22.93
CUSTOMER	On-Time-Delivery %	PM	65%	67%	-2%	
	SO Lines Delivered On-Time	PM	31	42	-11	
	SO Line Items Delivered Late	PM	17	21	-4	
	WIP Line Items Past Due (#)	PM	45	28	-17	
	WIP Line Items Past Due (%)	PM	12%	8%	4%	
	Warranty Returns (#)	RD	25	10	15	
	Warranty Costs (x1000)	LG	$ 143	$ 150	$ (7)	
	Warranty No Fault Found (#)	RD	1	1	0	
	Warranty No Fault Found ($)	RD	$ 4,000	$ 750	$ 3,250	
Internal	Overtime (DL) %	MF	5.2%	5.0%	0.2%	
	Kit OTD%	CD			0%	
	Supplier OTD (%)	CD	79%	89%	10%	
	Open Purchase Orders	CD	524	569	45	
	Past Due Purchase Orders	CD	53	45	8	
	SCAR's Open	JS	2	4	2	
	SCAR's Issued	JS	10	12	-2	
	SCAR's Closed	JS	10	12	-2	
	SCAR's Past Due	JS				
	Scrap ($)	MF	$17,400	$12,000	$5,400	
	NCR's Written	JS	95	111	-16	
	Squawks Written	JS	204	227	-23	
	Rework	MF	$6,400	$7,000	-$600	
	ERO's Released	LO	90	195	-105	
	ERO/ECO's Initiated	LO	476	505	-29	
	ECO's Released	LO	183	310	-127	
	Redlines Off the Floor	LO	94	145	-51	
	Total FT Employees	LM				
	Direct/Indirect Ratio	MF				
	Total Temps/PT/Contr.	LM				
	Open Employment Reqs	LM				
	Internal Audits Conducted	JS	11	11	0	
	External Audits Conducted	JS				
	CAR's Open	JS				
	CAR's Issued	JS	7	8	1	
	CAR's Closed	JS	12	15	3	
	CAR's Past Due	JS				
	Cost of Quality	MF			$ -	
	Housekeeping	CG				
	Safety	CG				
Invest	Training Hours	LM	12	15	-3	
	CAPEX	MF	$ 49,000	$ 125,000	$ 76,000	$ 125,000
	R&D	MF	$ -	$ 75,000	$ 75,000	$ 75,000

ACTION PLANS OR QUADS

Once the BSC is complete, we are then in a position to focus our attention as to where our process improvements or actions should be directed. That would be any metric that was listed as yellow or red on the BSC.

These BSC Action Plans are critical to the success of the organization's effort to *Go Forward*. "Go Forward. Always Go Forward." It was true of Patton and it's still true today. And the BSC and Action Plans will help put the focus on doing just that: *Going Forward!*

Without definitive Action Plans, focused specifically on the underperforming metrics, the process improvement actions are unfocused, unclear, and unowned and as such tend to fall by the wayside. I've seen many organizations where senior management mandates that certain items or metrics improve, but these efforts routinely fail due to the lack of a specific, well thought out, and defined Action Plan. In these cases, the Plan usually breaks down into a generic "Work Harder" approach and nothing improves. It doesn't improve because rarely is there a full understanding as to why the metric needs to improve or why it falls short and as such, we cannot effectively develop actions or a plan to fix it. The action ends up vague and unfocused. The premise here is that in order to fix a problem, you have to see it as a problem, fully understand the problem, and know what specifically is causing it.

I have found that for an Action Plan to be successful, there are four key elements that must be understood.

1. Metric: What it is we are trying to measure. I recommend that the metric not only provide a snapshot of what it is today, but also a historical look three to six months back, and provide a forward looking forecast for the next three to six months that will be the result of the action(s) being taken.

2. Drivers: The key contributors that feed, make up, or drive a particular metric. For instance, if you were tracking on-time delivery for a

manufacturing facility, the drivers may include items such as supplier on-time delivery, rework, machine down time, labor variance… These drivers are the basic elements that when added together make up the metric.

3. Issues: Items that directly relate to and contribute to the drivers. To use the on-time delivery scenario, issues here may include purchase orders to suppliers that are not placed on time and cause suppliers to be late. Or inadequate engineering for a particular component results in lost manufacturing time as the operations team sorts out the problems, and materials for some parts are hard to obtain, causing delays in getting the material to operations in time to make their schedule. Or Human Resources is having difficulty hiring qualified help, which causes added days to the schedule as the direct labor hours are stretched. The list goes on. These are all issues that affect our ability to deliver product on time to our customers. The key thing to keep in mind for defining issues is that they need to be very specific and measurable. For example, how do you measure "We need to do a better job ordering raw material"? Obviously that is not specific, but delivering all customer orders 98% on-time fits the model.

4. Action, Owner, and Completion Date: Now that you have a full understanding of the metrics, drivers and issues, it is time to discuss the action segment. Note that the action needs to have a direct correlation and impact on the issue. There needs to be a direct cause and effect relationship between the two. As an example, if an issue related to delivering product on time was that raw material does not arrive on time from our suppliers, then an action of ensuring that the raw material is ordered within the correct supplier lead time ties directly back to the issue. The action is linked and has a direct impact on that issue. An action of paying employees weekly versus the current method of every two weeks does not have an impact on the raw material issue. It may be an action, but it is not specifically related to the raw material issue and therefore in this case, is not a valid action.

Keep in mind that in order for the Action Plan to be successful, the actions should be made up of SMART actions. That is, they are: Specific, Measurable, Attainable, Realistic, and Timely.

Once the action has been identified, it is then necessary to assign an owner to that action. I find that designating or assigning a specific person responsible for the action is the best way to foster ownership, ensure follow through, and drive the accountability. Having an action with no one responsible for its accomplishment results in a lack of ownership and/or responsibility and the action fails or falls short of expectations. By putting a name on the action, you are in a much better position to drive the accountability for its completion. Patton knew specifically who was responsible for each portion of his Action Plans and he held his leaders accountable for the successful execution of those actions.

The last item is the Completion Date. This is the Timely aspect of the SMART Action. This also needs to be specific in order to establish the improvement timeline and also to ensure closure and the enhanced accountability. As an example, a completion date of May 15 is much more definitive than Second Quarter.

Using the same scenario for "purchase orders for suppliers are placed late," the action may be to reaffirm and adjust the supplier lead times or to develop a follow-up system to ensure that purchase orders are placed to suppliers on time in 95% of the cases by the buyers. Mary Smith will be responsible for this action and she will have it complete by May 15. Now the action meets the Specific, Measurable, Attainable, Realistic, and Timely definition. This is a major improvement over the action item that states that "All purchase orders need to be placed on time."

ACTION PLAN OR QUAD LAYOUT

When these four elements are understood, they would then be laid out into a one page Quad or Four Blocker arrangement:

1. Metric: Top Left

2. Drivers: Top Right

3. Issues: Bottom Left

4. Action, Owner, Completion Date: Bottom Right

This Quad would be set up landscape on an 8.5 x 11" sheet of paper. An example of the Quad layout is shown below:

Quad	
Metric	Drivers
Issues	Actions

Now that the Action Plan or Quad is prepared, it can easily be used as a tool to track progress not only on the Issues and Actions, but as to how these Actions remedy the Issues and drive the overall Metric improvement and who is responsible for it. The key here is to use this one page document as a tool and not a report. This is critical. Don't use the Action Plan as a month-end fill-out item or report. Use it as it was intended, a tool in day-to-day business activities. It is your roadmap, your plan. Use it effectively. It defines and highlights your tactics, what you are doing to remedy the underperforming metrics that are holding back the strategy.

To be effective this Action Plan concept used in conjunction with the Balanced Scorecard system needs to become part of the organizational culture. It will help provide the structure to ensure the strategy is deployed effectively. It also provides effective visual tools that I find are necessary when affecting an organizational culture change. An example of an Action Plan is given below:

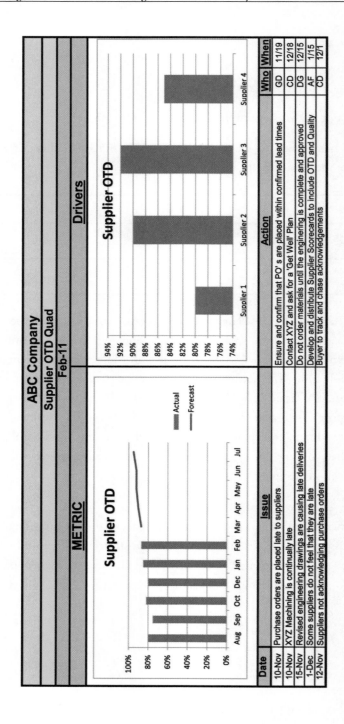

The Action Plan is a one page quad that is made up of the performance Metric, the related Drivers, Issues, and specific Actions related to rectifying the Issues and Drivers and providing a roadmap to improve the metric.

CONCLUSION – THE BUSINESS THREE A'S AND PERFORMANCE METRICS

By adopting this straightforward and no-nonsense approach, I feel that any organization can accelerate or improve its operational performance. I have successfully implemented these concepts and tools for several organizations and the results were major positive shifts in organizational performance.

A key point to remember here is that it is important to have an established and strong leadership, vision and strategy before attempting to implement alignment, actions and accountability. Without the development and implementation of these first, The Three A's do not have the foundation on which to stand.

I have always agreed with Patton's approach of keeping it simple and communicating what needs to be done, and his philosophy that you can't expect results if you don't plan, set the expectations, and provide the resources to accomplish those results. Many organizations are unclear as to the vision and strategy and find it difficult to gain any momentum. You must have these two elements in place in order establish alignment, action and accountability to be effective in *Moving Forward*.

Patton made it clear to everyone where he was going and how he was going to get there: his plan. "Know what you know and know what you don't know." He knew where he was going and in my career I've tried to do the same. I've strived to make it clear where the organization was going (vision), supplied the roadmap (strategy) and followed through with The Three A's to get there. This has been through planning, Balanced Scorecard development and implementation, monthly operating reviews, monthly all employee meetings, Incentive Compensation (Bonus) packages, and "walking the walk." All of it was developed and implemented to drive the organizational alignment, actions and accountability to *Move Forward*.

I literally lived the plans, giving 110% of my effort and support, much as Patton was heavily committed to making his plans a success.

The Three A's provide the method or tools to develop the tactics to implement the strategy. When metrics or alignment begin to slip, the actions correct them. These are the short term tactics: adjust, adapt and overcome. Once the alignment, actions and ownership are defined, you then have the means to hold and drive the organizational and personal accountability and the ability to *Move Forward*.

A BATTLE PLAN FOR THE BUSINESS THREE A'S AND PERFORMANCE METRICS

- **The Business Three A's (Alignment, Action and Accountability)**
  o Leadership, vision, and strategy need to be established before implementing the Business Three A's
  o Support and assist in the execution of the strategy
  o The Three A's complete the Six Elements of Business Success Pyramid
  o Set the organizational priorities, establish the expectations and needed follow through
  o **Alignment**
    ▪ A series of 3-5 objectives supporting the strategy for:
      - The Organization
      - Every department
      - Each employee
    ▪ Through this "bubbling up" process, each series of lower level objectives feeds and supports the next level
  o **Action**
    ▪ A clear and definitive set of actions (or steps) for each objective listed as part of the alignment process
      - A mini-strategy for meeting each objective

- Actions should be SMART

- Actions provide the necessary steps and related timelines to meet the objectives

o **Accountability**

- Define the expectations and consequences resulting from not meeting those expectations

- Reinforce the execution of strategic objectives and actions

- Incentive compensation provides the needed reward and reinforcement system

- **Performance Metrics**

o It is critical to understand the financials and how they interrelate

- Be able to explain the cause and effect relationships

- Ensure those on your leadership team understand the financials

- Look at not just the current numbers, but the trends as well

o **Balanced Scorecard (BSC)**

- A simple and effective one page document looking at four fundamental areas of the business:

  - Financial: financial statements

  - Customer: metrics from the customer perspective

  - internal Processes: areas that affect Customer and financial metrics

  - Investment: areas where organizational investment needs to be made to drive the other three functional areas green

- Each fundamental area has 3-10 specific metrics

- Metrics are color coded green, yellow, or red as measured against a forecast

- For each underperforming metric, an Action Plan (or Quad) should be developed

o **Action Plan (or Quad)**

- A simple one page document split into four areas that define the:

  - Metric

  - Driver

  - Issues

  - Actions, Owner, and Completion Date

CHAPTER 6
PATTON ON OPERATIONS

"Nothing is ever done twice."

General George S. Patton

Everything Patton did during the war was an operation. His landings and ground battle during Operation Torch in North Africa were operations. His time with General Pershing pursuing Pancho Villa, the battle at El Guettar, his landings in Sicily during Operation Husky and the following campaigns to take Palermo and Messina were all operations. Operation Fortitude, in which Patton commanded the decoy 1st U.S. Army Group in support of the Allied invasion of Normandy, Operation Cobra, his big drive and push across France to Germany, and his rescue of the 101st Airborne at Bastogne, were all operations.

This list would also include his large scale prewar maneuvers in the Carolinas, Texas and Louisiana as operations as well as the establishment of the Desert Training Center in California. There is long list of other operations. Everything Patton did was an operation. That was his focus, his center.

Patton believed that every operation must, as he put it, *"Go Forward! Always Go Forward!"* That means everything must function correctly and the activities and needs of that operation must be fully understood and supported in order to do so.

"Go Forward" means the troops are *Moving Forward*. As we've discussed, in order for that to happen, the operation needs to start with the vision and strategy followed with The Three A's: alignment, action and accountability to effectively *Move Forward*. With those items in place, the military operation now needs the support of:

- Housing Facilities
- Troops
- Transportation
- Intelligence

- Food and Water

- Ammunition

- Fuel

- Weapons

- Armament

- Medical

- Air cover

- Chaplain

And the list goes on. It included everything needed to support *Moving Forward* and the success of the operation. For Patton, everything centered on the operation. That was the focal point. That is what mattered: The operation. Everything supported the operation.

Think of the business as a wagon wheel with operations at the center; all other departments are at the outer ends of the spokes supporting the center hub–operations. These departments on the wheel rim revolve around the operations hub and are there to provide the support via the spokes allowing it to *Move Forward*.

Business and military operations function in much the same manner in that they are both about *Moving Forward*. A business is made up of several departments and these departments make up the elements of the operations support team. These support elements include: sales, business development, engineering, quality, supply chain, finance, and human resources. These support departments provide the orders, customer service, program management, new customers, new orders, new products, raw material, labor, process improvements, cost controls, overhead, cash flow, inventory, financials, etc. These items are considered operational support activities in and of themselves, and foster the ability of operations and the organization to continually function and *Move Forward*. Everything else is secondary to supporting operations.

Below is a diagram depicting how the organization should function in support of operations.

ORGANIZATIONAL WAGON WHEEL

Let's keep in mind that in business if operations is not delivering a product or service then it is just generating cost. If this is the case, it won't take long for the organization to go bankrupt as costs continue to exceed profitability. It's a simple concept: operations must produce if the organization is to generate sales, make a profit, and *Move Forward*.

As we discussed earlier, once the overall business strategy is developed and communicated, operations then needs to develop their own operations strategy or plan for how they will support the overall business strategy. This operations strategy or plan is the operational roadmap as to how they are going to get there.

This operations plan or strategy includes elements such as the requirements for direct labor, indirect labor, equipment, capital, raw material, supplies, capabilities, expertise, training, tooling, facilities, product flow, etc.—everything needed to support operations and the operations function in support of the overall strategy.

This operations plan should not be put together in a vacuum nor is it self supporting. It needs the support elements from other departments. Remember, all other departments are there to support operations and help it to *Move Forward*. Once this plan is complete, we've determined how we're going to get there. Now operations needs to execute and follow through on that plan. Again, the critical point here is that operations has their plan, and the other departments have their own plans that support operations in their drive to meet and support the overall organizational strategy. Operations cannot function on its own. Outside support for operations is crucial.

In the military it is important to keep the battle moving. For Patton, this meant keeping it fed with men, supplies, food, water, ammo, support, and equipment. The focus was to provide everything that the operation needed to keep it *Moving Forward*.

Businesses function in the same manner. We must always keep the production line or flow *Moving Forward*. We need to keep it fed with orders, raw material, manpower, equipment, tooling, facilities, and processes. That is its purpose and function.

I've worked with many organizations and have found some to be centered or focused on the sales, engineering, or finance departments and even some centered on HR or quality. What I have found is that as in Patton's battles, the operations department should be the center of the business. It should be the overall focal point of the entire organization. They are the ones that make the product, send it to customers, and generate invoices that pay the bills to keep the organization *Moving Forward*.

Operations is responsible for getting the product out the door once the order has been accepted, but they cannot do it on their own. They need the support of all the other departments in order to be successful. This is a critical concept and one that sometimes gets lost along the way. Sales, finance, HR, quality, essentially everyone else, are there to support operations and not the other way around.

This fundamental concept is lost in many organizations, holding back performance as a result. At times, operations is viewed as an engineering test lab where R&D activities take precedence over customer orders, taking resources and focus off the ability of operations to deliver product and *Move Forward*. In these cases the alignment is not correct, confusion results, and the accountability is lost as the organization sorts out what is really important. To be successful, everyone's job is to keep operations fed with orders, people, raw material, new products and delivery while the financials and the Balanced Scorecard highlight the progress.

Think of a business as a living being and operations as the heart. It has to keep pumping or the being dies. To make it go faster, it needs more food and oxygen. The same can be said about a business. To have operations produce and ship more product, it needs more orders and the capacity and resources to produce those orders. Again, to make it go faster and do more, you need to feed it what it needs to sustain itself at that pace. You can't climb Mt. Everest on 1,500 calories a day and you can't double the output of an operation without supplying an increase in orders and supporting resources, or the ability to increase its efficiencies.

PROCESS IMPROVEMENT

In business today, process improvement should be, but is not always, a consistent part of the normal course of our daily activities. We need to strive constantly to improve products, processes, efficiencies, and costs. In many organizations I routinely hear "we always do it that way" or "that always happens." As business leaders we should always strive to support process improvement ideas and activities to remedy the organization and rid it of those comments. Process improvement should be an integral part of our strategies and organizational culture.

Patton was always thinking of improvements to tactics, equipment, weapons, and training as with his recommendations for the tank in WWI and WWII, as well as the work he did on the cavalry saber, his training efforts with tanks, and his work at the Desert Training Center in southern California. There were many others including the Tankers uniform. One of his first leadership roles during WWI was with a process improvement initiative that improved the accounting for and marking of military vehicles in Paris. This was the forerunner of marking and stenciling on today's military vehicles.

In some cases Patton wrote directly to the War Department and in others he wrote directly to the manufacturers regarding his product improvement recommendations. It was part of his makeup. He was thinking about improvements all the time from both an efficiency standpoint and to protect his troops. He was always looking for efficiencies that would inflict the most amount of destruction to the enemy, with little damage to his troops.

Patton said his operations "are advancing constantly." It's true in battle as well as in the preparation for battle. He constantly thought about process improvements and in business we need to be doing the same thing. His motivation was trying to keep his troops safe in battle as he *Moved Forward*. In business, our motivation is to make more money.

Business improvements run the gamut from improvements to customer on-time delivery, labor and material efficiencies, standardization of products and sub-assemblies, capacity expansion, scrap reduction, and designs for manufacturability. Essentially, anything that can reduce cost, improve quality, reduce inventory, and accelerate throughput leading to higher shipments at a reduced overall cost.

As part of being efficient, Patton never wanted to retreat as he didn't want to expend resources going over the same ground twice. That was redundant and a waste of valuable resources. "Nothing is done twice," he said.

In business or manufacturing, this correlates to the cost of additional or unnecessary processing and lost capacity as the result of generating scrap and rework as part of the production process. This practice was unacceptable to Patton and should be unacceptable for businesses as well, but in many organizations these inefficiencies are accepted as a normal course of day to day operations. They just live with it. This is inefficient, costly, and consumes valuable resources that could be used on producing more product. These inefficiencies mean less throughput, more cost, and less profit potential.

I've never understood why some business leaders tolerate the old adage: "Why is there always enough time to do it over, but never enough time to do it right the first time?" If you take the time do it right the first time, you're actually done earlier and have saved money, time, and manufacturing capacity and pain. For me the reason this is allowed to happen is the lack of a real strategy and organizational misalignment as to what's important.

We cannot afford to maintain the status quo. Process improvement is part of the drive in *Moving Forward*. We need to be innovative, fix it, and *Move Forward*. It's all part of keeping operations fed and supported.

Ask the guy on the ground floor, or the foot soldier, for his process improvement ideas. He'll tell you what needs to be fixed or addressed. Listen to him. He'll have lots of thoughts and ideas and in almost every instance, he's right. But in many cases he doesn't feel anyone listens.

CONCLUSION - OPERATIONS

Over the years in handling operations, I've learned to always have a plan and have been able to adjust that plan to fit the situation. Patton's philosophy was the same: "Strategy and tactics do not change; only the means of applying them is different."

Even in change, he stuck with those core principles: "One must choose a system and stick to it." Putting and keeping the organizational focus on operations is part of the strategy and system and I've strived to pick a specific operational course of action and stick to it despite roadblocks and interference. Patton had the same concept and has been quoted as saying "Leadership is not a popularity contest," and that a leader must "be willing to make decisions. That's the most important quality in a good leader." I agree and have functioned under both of these premises.

In the handling of a turnaround, you are there to make a major impact on the performance of that business, sometimes after it has already reached critical mass. I've been chastised for not going around roadblocks in my path, and having a tendency to go right through them.

Change does not come easily and it has a price. Over the years, many if not all of the comments regarding my operational approach have come from the middle management ranks of the organization in need of turnaround. In many cases these managers did not have the experience, background, or ability to function in a turnaround mode. It was through their efforts, or non-efforts, that the organization found itself in its predicament. I asked for improvement, set the direction, and helped in the preparation of the plan, but nothing *Moved Forward* because, often, they literally did not know how to do it. The result was the same old status quo. When I've stepped in and implemented a new, innovative, or controversial way to get the things moving, they didn't like it. I've never apologized for any of the actions taken because I believe that they were right for the time and place. As Patton said, "You need to overcome the tug of people against you as you reach for high goals."

As part of my operational turnaround experiences, I've been faced with serious customer delivery and cash flow issues that needed immediate action. In these situations, when not getting any internal action or support to remedy the issue, and with a lack of response to coaching, I've been known to adopt a somewhat directive style and made some tough decisions that some disliked. My explanation was that I viewed these situations with the same measure of urgency as a house fire. I didn't have the time to gather everyone around and ask their opinion as to whether or not we needed to put the fire out or how we should put it out. The bottom line was that the house was on fire and I took action to put it out.

I have also been chastised for the intensity and accelerated pace at which these operational turnarounds have been accomplished. Like Patton, in several cases I've come at them in a bold and audacious manner. Some were intense. When working with an aircraft refurbishing company that was retrofitting a large number of aircraft for a major freight carrier, some members of the management team did not feel the need or have the commitment to meeting the customer or senior leadership timelines and expectations. The task was huge and we were given some very aggressive delivery requirements. Certain members of the management team were not aligned, and questioned my leadership, strong commitment, and drive to complete the project on time. The direction was set, the plan prepared and executed resulting in all of the aircraft delivered on time.

Once, I was tasked with turning around another organization but without upsetting anyone in the process. "How do I do that?" I had the courage to hold my ground and needless to say there were conflicts and confrontations along the way. But the plan was developed, the actions were taken, and the organization grew well over 200% during the next two years. The plan was put together and successfully executed and the rewards and benefits speak for themselves. If you're going to make scrambled eggs, you are going to have to break the yolks.

In other operational turnaround situations, there were members of the staff and mid-management that did not see the need to change how they were operating. They were indifferent and refused to change despite the coaching and mentoring, the old passive resistance routine. When some were removed from their positions for performance (accountability) and alignment issues, some in the organization were shocked. However, with the resistance removed, organizational performance picked up dramatically and the business *Moved Forward*.

In another situation, I was in the midst of an interview with a personnel director who did not agree with my performance improvement approach and accountability philosophy. She told me that by today's standards I had dinosaur values and that the failure of an employee to perform was not his responsibility. It was mine. Needless to say, I didn't get the position.

Patton said: "Lead me, follow me or get out of my way," and "You need to overcome the tug of people against you as you reach for high goals." And I have done that as well in my past. Patton put up with a lot of negativity for his drive, passion, and enthusiasm during his operations in Sicily and France and he took it in stride despite having his own internal self doubt.

I too have received external criticisms for my operational turnaround strategies and tactics, but those turnarounds were successful. We both had the courage to state our convictions about what needed to be done, take a stand, and successfully execute the strategy and tactics. I've stuck with a "back to basics" strategy.

Stay focused on the operation– that's where it all happens. Strive to execute the plan and keep operations fed. And above all, *"Go Forward! Always Go Forward!"*

A Battle Plan for Operations

- Primary Premise: Operations is the functional center of the organization
  - o Everything revolves around and supports operations
  - o All other departments need to align themselves to support operations
  - o If product is not being produced, then the operation is not *Moving Forward*
- When the vision and overall strategy are in place, operations then develops their own 3-5 objectives that support the overall business objectives
- Once these objectives are established, operations then develops their own operations plan
  - o This plan includes the needed labor, material, facilities, equipment, tooling, processes, procedures, capital, other support and resources needed to meet the operations plan
  - o Keep the plan simple and communicate it throughout the organization

o Track, measure, and report your progress

  ▪ Prepare Action Plans for areas that are underperforming

- For operations to accelerate or expand throughput it will require more resources or the ability to improve efficiencies

- Process Improvement is a key component to effectively *Move Forward*

  o Fix the operational processes so that "Nothing is done twice"

    ▪ Strive to reduce scrap and rework

  o Take the time and provide resources to remedy inefficiencies

    ▪ To include labor and material

  o Listen to those folks on the shop floor; They have excellent ideas for improvements

CHAPTER 7
PATTON ON SALES AND MARKETING

"America loves a winner and will not tolerate a loser,
this is why America has never lost and will never lose a war."

"Nobody ever defended anything successfully.
There is only attack, attack and attack some more."

George S. Patton

D-Day was June 6, 1944. It marked the long awaited Allied invasion of Europe. General Patton was to lead the mission dubbed Operation Overlord on the shores of France at the Pas de Calais with American, British, and Canadian forces.

Or that's what German intelligence thought. Patton instead was in command of a fictitious decoy force and the main thrust of the invasion was on the beaches of Normandy, far from Patton and his empty boats. It was "advertised" through an aspect of Operation Fortitude, a deception strategy for Overlord, and "sold" to the Germans that Patton was to lead the invasion and that he would invade at Pas de Calais. The Germans were convinced that Patton was to lead the battle as they believed that Patton was the greatest U.S. general. This deceptive "advertising" reinforced that belief. To them it made perfect sense.

This deception effort was a ruse aimed at holding the German troops north at Pas de Calais and well away from the real invasion further south at Normandy. It worked very well and, even as the invasion had begun, Berlin was still convinced that the real invasion would come at Pas de Calais and that it would be led by Patton. The Germans knew him well and they were afraid of him. This deception (or strategic advertising) worked and allowed the Allies to gain a strong foothold in Normandy.

As early as October 1943 the Germans were convinced that Patton was to lead the invasion. The U.S. established a fictitious 1st U.S. Army Group (FUSAG) under Patton and placed it in Dover across from Pas de Calais. The U.S. Army used a multitude of deceptive techniques such as rubber trucks, aircraft, tanks, plywood artillery, dummy troop concentrations, and false radio traffic to make it appear that the 1st U.S. Army Group was real. Patton was stationed near there just outside Knutsford and the Germans knew it. He once said that it's "better to fight for something than to die for nothing," which may not seem fitting for a general in charge of a decoy ploy. However, the success of Operation Fortitude as part of the Overlord Strategy was a contributing factor in the success of the D-Day invasion, another example of a supporting plan or strategy.

PATTON AND MARKETING

Patton's G2, his intelligence unit, performed the equivalent of business market research.

A very well respected unit, his G2 was very capable and in several cases knew more of what was going on with the enemy and their activities than any other agency, including Supreme Headquarters Allied Expeditionary Force, or SHAEF. Patton insisted on honest, accurate, and real time intelligence regarding the location of the enemy (or, in business speak, his competition), his strength, and his potential activities.

Patton knew the benefits of a well thought-out and executed sales and marketing campaign or plan. He routinely marketed himself and his accomplishments in the quest to fulfill his vision, and his self-promotion extended to military and personal connections. Patton frequently wrote letters about his activities to anyone he felt could help him (today we call it networking), such as General Pershing, Eisenhower, Bradley, Cunningham, even his wife's father, a successful and wealthy textile mill owner. He would send letters offering his opinions and suggestions to his superiors, peers, and subordinates, as well as offering congratulations on their achievements or actions. He was a general/ salesman and knew how to network.

While he was busy with his operations in Africa and Europe, Patton had a very strong and influential ally and spokesperson in Washington: his wife, Beatrice.

Bea, as she was called, routinely assisted in his self-promotion during the war. She was a loving, loyal, and supportive wife, his number one supporter who worked hard at providing that support. She understood everything about him and during her war bond tours did whatever she could to promote her Georgie and his image. She took a backseat to his fame and was happy to do it. Patton's career was about him and not her.

Being the wife of a senior officer, Bea was "plugged in" to the military and political networks of the capital. She had her connections, as well. The Pattons were well known in the Washington military and political social circles and Bea worked her connections and networked in support of her husband.

Bea was also pursued by the media, frequently granting interviews where she would lobby for full support of her husband and strive to protect his image and reputation on the home front. She was very instrumental in the publication of two popular articles; one in *Life Magazine* titled "Life of General Patton" and another in *Readers Digest* titled "Old Man Battle."

Bea had her finger on Washington's pulse and provided feedback to Patton as to the local gossip regarding his activities, frequently sending the general interesting news clippings of him and his accomplishments. She was instrumental in reaffirming and supporting her husband's efforts. You could say that Bea was his U.S./D.C. ambassador and actively spoke supporting his thoughts, ideas, and actions. Or that she was his biggest public relations manager and salesman. She was good at it. At the time, other senior military wives were doing their share of networking. When I was in the U.S. Navy, the squadron wives also did their fair bit of networking and I've seen this in the business world as well. It's part of the selling process. They were all representing and selling for their husbands.

Patton was a favorite with the media. He was larger than life with his flamboyant personality, his sometimes profane language, his passion, and his impeccable uniform right down to the ivory handled pistols. He was an actor and played the part well and the news media ate it up. Patton actually had sirens installed on his command car so everyone knew he was coming. He was a showman and looked and acted the part. As mentioned earlier, Patton was a poet and a poem of his was published in the Women's Home Companion titled "God of Battles." He received $50 for that piece.

Patton may seem to have been a media hound, but he was picky and very concerned about his image and what information would become public. In February 1942, Patton got wind that *Life* was going to publish an article about him that his superiors thought detrimental. Patton worked to have the story pulled.

Life and *Time* magazines were preparing articles about Patton in November 1942 just after the landings in North Africa. Patton was again concerned about the articles and worked to have them blocked. These articles contained what he thought were "several objectionable features" that he felt were not true, stating to the editors that "the above remarks are highly detrimental." They were not in his best interest, potentially putting him in a bad light, thus taking focus away from his efforts and troops.

Patton's well circulated image in his polished, unblemished uniform served him well with his networking and with the media. Knowing the value of the press, he worked to control and sell his image his way.

When Germany declared war on France in August 1914, Patton wrote to General Wood, the General of the Eastern Department, marketing himself and requesting a one year leave of absence to go and fight with the French. Forgoing a company "expense report" (in corporate terms), Patton even offered to cover the expenses out of his own pocket! He knew he needed to do that in order to make himself known.

He was self promoting with a vision in mind and that vision was to be a Great Military Leader. Very early in his career he was promoting and marketing his thoughts and ideas by writing several articles for military periodicals. These efforts helped him to become a known entity. During WWII, he marketed himself and his troops with press conferences, all too happy to toot his own horn. He would continually look at the media feedback as to how he was doing in the public eye, both personally and regarding his troops as a whole.

SALES & MARKETING IN BUSINESS

By definition, a customer is a current or potential buyer of our goods or services. In business today, we need to believe and follow through on the premise that the "Customer is #1," or the old adage, "if we don't take care of our customers, someone else will."

In many cases today this concept is lost. As an example, when you call the customer service or sales department of an organization, how often do you get a "live" person on the telephone? Nine times out of 10 you will end up with a recording that says "For sales, press one," and after about three of these routings, we say "enough of this" and hang up. Heck, I've called some businesses, but I didn't know the name of the person or the extension, only the department and I've found it impossible to get anyone on the line to help me! Frustrating, yet it happens every day in businesses all over the country.

We must remember: Customers are not the enemy, though at times I've seen them treated and referred to as such. In business today, we've lost the entire "taking care of the customer" mentality and it's just not right. In some instances customers are viewed as a nuisance and not as an opportunity and that attitude needs to change if we are going to be successful at *Moving Forward*. Think about this: Have you been to the Department of Motor Vehicles (DMV) lately? How's that for a customer service model?

Patton's customers were SHAEF, the War Department, the President, the general public, and the forces he supported. He "sold" his services and activities to them. Think of it this way: What would have happened to Patton if he didn't provide his customers with quality service? He'd be out of a job!

In today's business world, there are two sets of customers: internal customers and external customers.

Internal customers include the board of directors, corporate, those folks "upstairs," management, our peers, other internal departments, and our subordinates. It could also be looked at very simply as the next person or department in the chain of a process. For example, "we do this work for the contracts department," or, "we prepare this report and send it to corporate," or, "we put this subassembly together and send it over to the final assembly area to get installed in the final unit." They are our internal customers; we do or process something for them.

Another example would be that the quality department inspects a process operation or product to ensure it has been done correctly. In this case, operations is the customer.

Engineering designs a component or product for operations. Purchasing orders the raw material for operations. Human resources hires the employees to support operations. In all of the above cases, operations is the customer. Do you see the pattern here? All of these departments are supporting their customer: operations.

External customers are people or businesses for whom we actually make a product or supply a service. Tom Peters sold a lot of books in the 1980s about how to take care of the customer. He said that we sell to customers and not markets. He was right. A lot of people say that we sell this to the ABC market or we sell this to the aerospace market. As Tom Peters said, "I've never known a market to buy anything." I know customers that buy things, but never a market.

Another business customer is the general public, which creates our public image. How does it look out there? How are we doing with the regulatory agencies as we strive to keep a good, strong company image out there in the marketplace? As part of that image, how are we doing in taking care of the environment? Patton knew his public image very well and worked hard to build and maintain it. In business, we need to do the same.

In both cases, in order to be successful and *Move Forward*, we must keep the customer satisfied, happy, and content.

Patton kept the customer satisfied by his performance on and off the battlefield. He was always striving for more responsibility, more troops, and more opportunity to lead a major offensive and he knew that in order for that to happen he needed to take care of his customers: the folks "upstairs."

In business, it's important to keep the customer satisfied with our performance by supplying a quality product, on time and at a reasonable price with professional customer service. Keeping the customer satisfied means that we have either met or exceeded his expectations.

By doing this we are able to increase sales. I have done it and it set the stage for both personal and organizational growth with new investment, added responsibility, raises and promotions for both internal and external customers.

Just think about your reaction after you've experienced a less than optimum outcome during a sales transaction: Do you go back to that restaurant, department store, or car dealership and do it again? Or, do you seek a better and more pleasurable experience elsewhere? If you were not happy where you were, you're naturally going to go find a suitable and more customer friendly experience. That is the reality of not taking care of the customer. They leave and go to your competition.

We cannot be all things to all people; neither can a business. Businesses should stay focused on their core competencies and work from that strength. That is why, from a military perspective, we have an Army, Navy, Marine Corps, and Air Force. They all have their strengths in particular areas. Business is the same. That is part of the business strategy. It is defining the targeted customers and our product offerings—we can't do everything for everybody. Stick with what you do best. Stay focused on what you know and exhaust all those possibilities before you jump into something that is new and different.

Once the expertise and products are defined, it's time to really get to know the targeted customers: who they are, what they want or need, what are their issues, what causes them pain, and how can we help them fulfill their needs and get rid of their pains? Customers buy because they have a need and we should fully understand how we can fulfill that need. This is a critical and fundamental element of sales. As Tom Peters said: "Find a niche and meet a market."

We as businesses need to tailor our products and services to fit their needs in order to make a sale. We need to meet their expectations and make it easy, both from a product and service level. To understand this, we need to listen,

listen, and listen some more. If you listen, *really listen*, they will tell you what they need. We need to stay in close contact with the customer. Or as Tom Peters always asked, do you really *smell* the customers and understand what it is that they want?

Another thing to keep in mind is that people buy based on emotion and they buy from people they trust and respect. You have always heard comments such as "that guy is nothing but a used car salesman." Being viewed as a "used car salesman" is not the image you want to have in the military or in the business world. Trust and integrity are key concepts in both arenas. Patton worked hard to build and maintain his image and we need to do the same both personally and in business. You need to have that trusting win-win relationship in order to be successful and develop strong customer rapport. While striving for that trusting, win-win relationship, we need to continually work together with our customers to solve their issues and problems. We need to remember that it's all about the customer and his needs. Not ours.

In too many cases, I have seen salesmen use a cookie-cutter, one size fits all approach. He has a standard selling routine or speech and that is not what the customer wants to hear. He is not listening to the customers; he's pitching. Often, customers buy an off the shelf item only to modify it to fit their needs. For your targeted customers, you should understand this aspect of your products and work with the customer to remedy it: Understand his needs and strive to fulfill them. Provide a meaningful service and you'll both win.

UNDERSTANDING THE COMPETITION

Knowing your competition is just as critical in business as it is in the military. In the military, we need to know all about the enemy—their location, concentration, weaponry, what does G2 or intelligence say they are about to do, where are they going, who is leading the organization, and what are his tactics and strengths and weaknesses. In wartime, if you don't know the size, make up, capability, and location of your enemy, people could be killed.

Patton did continual research about his enemy, his tactics, equipment, and leadership strengths and weaknesses. He understood each of these items so he could exploit the weaknesses while staying away from the strengths. He also did a lot of reading about who he was up against in battle. He actually read the German General Rommel's book *Infantry Attacks* regarding his WWI experience and the tactics employed during the war. (This was noted in the movie "Patton" during the El Guettar battle when Patton yells, "Rommel you magnificent bastard, I read your book!" The story was right, but the movie had the book title wrong). This gave Patton an excellent advantage in understanding how Rommel thought and made him more predictable. He understood his enemy. Patton knew that if he wanted to win, then he had to fully understand his opponent and anticipate his moves. He did an excellent job of it.

In the military, reconnaissance and research tell you all about the enemy. Understanding your enemy (or in our case, the competition) is crucial in winning battles. Business is the same way.

In business, I'm amazed at the lack of understanding regarding competitors today. Marketing in business is the same as the G2 or Intelligence departments in the military. Marketing is where you gain the "intel" on your competition. I can't tell you how many times when being brought a customer quote for approval, I'll ask simple questions like "who is the competition?" "What are their strengths and weaknesses?" "What are they offering?" "What's their price?" "Who is the sales person?" "What is the market?"

These are standard questions as I try to understand the situation. I am just amazed that I am routinely met with "I don't know" or the classic "The buyer said the target price is $XXX and if we match it we'll get the order." And these comments usually come from the director of sales or sales manager! To me this is shameful and irresponsible. Just as in battle, understanding your competition is critical to *Moving Forward* and *Accelerating Performance*.

Who are they, where are they, what is their core business, what markets are they in, what are their annual sales, what do they make, are they profitable, what's their strategy, where are they going, have you done a SWOT (Strengths,

Weaknesses, Opportunities, and Threats) analysis? Do they have a union, have they been in the news, what's the scuttlebutt in the marketplace, where and how do we compete, any expansion plans, who's in charge, what's his/her background, are they private or publicly traded?

We need to fully understand our opponent just as Patton understood his. You should have a file on every one of your competitors with any information you can get your hands on and it should be up to date. When I've inquired about acquiring this competitor information, the first reaction I usually get is that the information is not available. Then the sales manager or the salespeople look at me and say, "That is just impossible. We can't gather up that much information." That is the wrong answer and the wrong attitude. It all goes back to the strategy and corresponding alignment, actions and accountability.

In today's world, the Internet is full of information, good and bad. Google is your friend. Use it! There is a vast amount of information out there on the Internet, whether it is on websites, Linkedin, Facebook, Twitter, press releases, awards, news articles, court or civic actions. It's all out there waiting for you to just go and get it.

I'm also surprised at what some companies put out on their websites: You'll see the size of their facility, organizational charts, photos of their new and latest technology piece of equipment with comments regarding its fantastic capabilities, as well as photos of their products and in some cases proprietary tooling and processes all posted on the website or in a brochure. They publish a wealth of information that really shouldn't be there! But if it's out there, it's fair game! Use it!

Patton said, "Know what you know and know what you don't know," and I'll add to that: Once you know what you don't know, go find it out! Do your own reconnaissance, your own intelligence gathering. People love to talk about themselves. Go to tradeshows. Be audacious and ask direct questions, take photos of their product, their booth, and their people. It's there, go for it! Pick up their literature. It's out on the table—take one. Some companies bring junior and inexperienced people to tradeshows to give them some experience.

They are excellent sources for information. Get them cornered and away from the rest of the group and they'll love to talk and tell you what it is they know—take advantage of their eagerness.

Question customers and suppliers about your competition. Obviously you need to be low key about how you ask, whether they are casual meetings or talking with a salesman, or you're at lunch, or out at the golf course. Again, people like to tell you what they know. Ask and you'll be surprised what people will tell you.

Here's one that I really like. Call your competitor and tell the receptionist that you are updating your customer database and would like to ask her a few questions. As you start asking away, you'll be shocked at what you'll learn.

There was an old poster from WWII: "Loose Lips Sink Ships." It's still true today, because people love to talk. The bottom line is that if you're going to be successful in business (or in battle), you must know and understand your competition completely and thoroughly! In today's information age, there is no excuse for poor intelligence or G2 on your competition.

As a side note, now that you've done this reconnaissance and research, take a look at what's out on the Internet about you and your organization. Trust me, you'll be surprised. Then take a look at your own website. Do you really want all that detail and information out there? What information do your people share at tradeshows and with suppliers? Do they talk too much and provide too much information? What would your receptionist tell someone who calls out of the blue and starts asking questions? Would she talk too much and provide sensitive information?

Think about this: If we are smart enough to go find out information on them, then they are finding out information on us; It's competition.

THE SALES PLAN

Today I don't often see a structured approach to selling. Most organizations may have a loosely defined sales plan, but it usually lacks the granularity as to what their market is, who their target customers are, and what products and services they are going after. They do not have a structured sales plan or a strategy and as such are missing opportunities and sales.

When you ask what the sales strategy is, you get a generic "Well, we make XXX for the ABC market folks." When you try to narrow it down, it gets a bit more specific but is still relatively loose. If they can't tell you what the sales strategy is, then they don't have one.

Most of these sales plans lack clarity as to what they are really going after. Salesmen don't understand their markets or their customers. They operate in a reactionary mode, quoting or responding to what comes their way. There is no real plan. There isn't a list of targeted customers or products. Or a calling schedule or corresponding customer action plans. I get frustrated when I read a salesman's rambling trip report and read the words, "Follow up in two weeks." Follow up on what? What are you going after? What are you selling and what's your plan to close the sale?

When I talk about a structured sales strategy, in aerospace that equates to targeting specific components or products on specific aircraft platforms. For instance, part of the strategy may be to obtain a contract for the motors assemblies that drive the back-up hydraulic system on the military C17 aircraft. Or to obtain a contract or teaming arrangements to develop a new component repair with ABC Company for the stage 1 turbine blades of the PW4000 engine. That approach is targeted and specific in nature. That structured approach to selling is missing today. There is a lack of a clearly defined plan.

Some salespeople out there will sell to anyone, anywhere. There really isn't a strategy other than "we're going to increase sales X percent next year," but it isn't clear where those current sales or new business sales are really going to come from or how they are going to do it. There is a lack of clarity about what the target market, customer, and product really are. That is not a strategy.

There should be a lot of discussion and a lot of thought about what's really in the sales funnel (or pipeline) and where those potential orders are in the sales cycle. What is really going to be booked as an order and when? In many cases, this funnel or pipeline activity is not well documented. It's all in the salesman's unstructured head as he goes about his unstructured and reactionary day. As a result, his efforts are unclear, unfocused, vague, and most often unsuccessful.

We need to understand what issues need to be resolved in order to close a sale. What do we need to do to close the sale? Again it goes back to the action plan: What's the plan? How are we going to close the sales? How do we expect to win if we don't have a plan?

I've seen many cases where there may be a loosely defined sales-strategic focus, but when a big RFQ (Request for Quotation) comes in and it really doesn't fit the strategy (the almighty homerun), we rationalize it and quote it anyway. I call it the "shoot anything that moves" or "shotgun" strategy. There really isn't a plan and we go after anything. The salespeople and even the director or VP will go after anything—the bigger the better. Gotta meet the quota!

To me, this approach wastes precious resources that would be better utilized on quoting work that actually fits the overall strategy and the core capabilities of the business. We need to develop the plan, stick to the plan, and then follow through with the plan. This is the best way to, as Patton said, "Accept the challenges so that you can feel the exhilaration of victory."

In a lot of cases this goes back to the lack of a clearly defined organizational vision and strategy that we talked about earlier. The strategy is vague and unclear and as a result, the focus and direction of the sales strategy is vague and unclear. Or it may be that orders (or the salesman quota) are down and we drastically need to find something, put it in the funnel and pull it through in order to book the sale. The old "We have to get the numbers up" approach. This breaks down into salesman survival mode, as I call it, as he struggles to keep the orders flowing (or just meeting his quota) and goes after anything and everything. Again with the shotgun, "Shoot anything that moves!" just to hit our numbers! This hard-core concept was discussed earlier in the Three A's segment when we talked about organizational alignment, action and accountability. The same holds true for the sales organization.

THE QUOTING PROCESS

Let's remember that whatever is sold to the customer, the operations folks must manufacture or produce. Therefore it is imperative that operations be involved at the earliest point in the development phase in order to provide the necessary insight and guidance into its manufacturability, meaning how it is going to be made, how much it's going to cost, and how long it's going to take. They need to be part of the initial engineering process up front.

This includes not only how the pieces will be put together, but also the materials used, the material properties, availability and costs, processing techniques, inspection and testing operations, the entire flow.

If done in unison and with a cooperative effort, it will eliminate or significantly reduce any surprises down the road. It's teamwork. Regardless of what was sold to the customer and at what price, operations will be the ones who "make or break" the outcome. Get them involved early. They have good, valuable, and needed input for the success of the program. Use them.

Another quoting shortfall resulting from the lack of a real sales strategy is the organizational alignment. Too many times I have seen the sales department get a large RFQ and independently quote a price and delivery to the customer without interfacing with any other department in the organization. They exclude the valuable input from operations, engineering, finance, quality… everyone. They just put a number together and send it to the customer. Then, when the company wins the order, the operations, engineering, and finance folks are frustrated, confused, and upset because they are unable to meet the requirements (cost and delivery) of the order. You cannot put a quote together without input and buy-in from the rest of the organization.

The result is that the order is late, costs were higher than projected, we lose money, and the customer is unhappy. The only one who is happy is the sales person because he got the order, made his quota, and probably received his commission. Remember: "An Army is a team…" Business is the same way. It's a team.

See anything wrong with this approach? Where was the plan or process? Nothing is tied together, nothing flows, and there is no alignment or teamwork. Only frustration, excess cost, and falling short of the customers' expectations. Again strategy, alignment, action and accountability all need to work together to fulfill the vision.

A structured quoting process includes all aspects of the organization, taking into account the organization's capabilities, facilities, resources, costs, material availability, and so on. The entire organization (the team) buys into it and approves the quote. We all agree that we can do this for $XXX in ABC time frame. It's not just prepared in a vacuum and sent to the customer. It's an all for one and one for all approach.

Another aspect of quoting is that if the customer wants a particular product for $XX and we cannot make it at a profit selling it for $XX, then we should walk away or work with him to command a higher price based on the value offered and his needs. In many situations that doesn't happen. Just to "get the order" we rationalize costs with various (and some unfounded) assumptions, lower our selling price, win the order, and then wonder why we didn't make money on the order. It is critical to understand the entire "big picture" and set your "walk-away" price and then have the courage, strength, or audacity to walk away. It's a tough decision, but one that will pay big dividends down the road. I'd rather make and deliver a product that I can make a profit on and not one where I'll lose money. It's a simple concept, but one that is often lost in the organization's drive to win orders.

Remember the earlier discussions regarding organizational vision, strategy, alignment, action and accountability. These are key components of the new production process as well as how we arrive at the customer selling price. Have the courage to set and stay the course. Develop the sales strategy and stick to it.

The quoting and new order reward system is also structured. Salespeople should not be just rewarded on the sale; they should be rewarded on the profitability of the sale and collections after the sale as well as the booking of the sale itself. It is teamwork. It's alignment, action, and accountability and it needs to be rewarded as such.

To be clear, sales departments should not be solely rewarded for slashing price and cutting lead times just to get the order. It shouldn't work that way. They are a part of the entire process (not THE process) and a part of the entire business, not just the beginning of the process.

By the same token, operations should be rewarded not only for shipments and shipment profitability, but also for booking new orders as they too are part of the entire business process. It doesn't do anybody any good to win business if the operations people cannot produce the product and deliver it on time, so the business can make money. Operations folks also need to be graded and/or rewarded for obtaining new work. They should have just as much skin in the game as the sales team.

A DIFFERENT APPROACH: STRATEGIC SELLING

Let's assume the company vision and strategy are clearly defined. The sales plan is thoroughly prepared and structured with specific and detailed monthly sales targets, targeted customers, and products. Think specific objectives or targets. They are there and it's clear where we are going.

For example, let's say that I'm going deer hunting in Nacona, TX, the week of November 15, for three days and plan to bag a buck with a 30-06 rifle. That objective is pretty clear and specific. Instead of "I am going to go deer hunting sometime this fall."

Once the sales plan is complete it's time to prepare specific and defined action plans for each customer and specific sales objectives for that particular customer. You may have three or four opportunities with that customer. What you want to do is to have defined action plans for each of those customer opportunities. This includes lots of information related to who, what, how, where, and when the sale will actually close. Consider this list:

- What problem is the customer trying to solve?
- How much information do we have regarding the potential order?
- What don't we know and how do we get that information?

- Who is the competition and how do we stack up?
- How do we exploit or better our position?
- Who within the organization makes the overall decision?
  - o What influence do the Economic, and Technical buyers have in the ultimate "buy" decision?
  - o How much do we know about them and what are they seeking out of the sale?
  - o What will they get from the sale?
    - Is it a promotion or potential promotion that they may get?
    - Do they get a bonus?
    - Or do they just get brownie points?
- Who within the organization is our Coach and what are his "wins" in the sale?
- Who within the organization is against us?
  - o Who, why, and how do we win over?
  - o What are their "wins" in the process?
    - What do they get out of giving or not giving us the order?
- What can we do to fix it or reinforce our position within that organization?
- What are the next steps?

Again it's the beginning elements of a roadmap or a comprehensive list of things we need to know on our journey to close the sale.

Once you've compiled all this information (including what you don't know) you're then in a position to develop a detailed and structured action plan specific to that sale or customer. This will be your plan, your strategy and roadmap to closing the sale. You need to have the discipline to use it, update it, and live it. This structured action plan will be your key to closing a successful sale. The customer sales action plan needs to be specific, structured, detailed, and to the point.

Another aspect of strategic selling is in forging an alliance with targeted customers. In this realm, you are functioning as an extension of their organization. You are there to offer assistance and help them solve a problem. Get yourself in on the ground level of the project. Once the RFQ comes out, it's too late. Become an integral part of the development process, the earlier in the process the better.

I have found the Miller Heiman Strategic Selling model to be ideal. Their book, *The New Strategic Selling*, and corresponding training seminars are excellent tools. I have been able to use them very effectively.

COMMUNICATION: INTERNAL AND EXTERNAL

Patton had a very clear understanding of what it took to sell himself, his troops, and their accomplishments and he always strived to be the best at what he did. He was a master at communication. He was not bashful about his self promotion. He thought he was the best and he was going to let everyone know he was the best. His statement that "All very successful commanders are prima donnas and must be so treated" fits this application very well. He had a very strong sense of what it meant to be a successful communicator and he was good at it.

His official reports to SHAEF as well as his informal letters, press conferences, and media briefings were well done, polished, and professional and fit with his brand.

This was all part of his sales and marketing campaign for himself and his troops: He was proud of himself and of them. In quite a few cases he was very audacious in his exploits just so he could make a big splash for himself. For example, look at his exploits in Sicily with his drive to Palermo and then on to Messina, beating General Montgomery. This was done not only to gain recognition and support for himself, but also to show the British and the world the abilities, capabilities, drive, expertise, and courage of the U.S. soldier and leadership. From a business perspective, he knew his troops were a better supplier than Monty and the Brits! He communicated, "sold," and delivered on that image. We need to do the same.

At Bastogne during the Battle of the Bulge, he made a big impression by rescuing the 101st Airborne. Again, this highlighted not only his abilities, but also those of his 3rd Army.

Just under two months after the Normandy landings, Patton took command of the U.S. 3rd Army in France on August 1, 1944. His mission was to assist in Operation Cobra, a massive drive out of the Normandy hedgerow area and then a rapid advance across France toward Germany to end the war. Patton Moved Forward aggressively, covering a vast amount of territory in a short amount of time, gaining press coverage, publicity, and notoriety along the way.

In business, it is the same: We have to communicate and sell ourselves. That is, to continually market and sell ourselves and our organizations to our customers. Communication is the key. Like it or not we are in a competition, both personally and business-wise. May the best man or organization win.

Be active: ask customers how you're doing and listen carefully to what you hear. This is a critical concept that is sometimes lost today. Remember that 90% of effective communication is listening. A common pitfall happens before the customer even speaks: We have already made up our minds, because we think we already know what he wants or what he is going to say. That is what I call "already listening" before the customer speaks. Salesmen are great at hearing what they want to hear and not necessarily what is being said. How can you help? Listen to what is being said.

I've often heard that a particular customer was unhappy and dissatisfied with the level of service received and he provided some very candid and open feedback. When I asked the sales people about the comment, I was told that the customer didn't know what he was talking about and that he was wrong or off base with his feedback. I found this a very interesting response. Doesn't he realize that a customer's perception of our service *is* the customer's reality? This attitude, whether it comes from sales or anywhere else in the organization, highlights a major disconnect in the "taking care of the customer" mantra. It's an alignment, action, and accountability shortfall that needs to be addressed if you expect to *Move Forward* or *Accelerate Performance*.

INTERNAL COMMUNICATION

Our communication about what we have been up to is handled through weekly or monthly reports, conference calls, memos, e-mails, and meetings. How we are doing goes back to the financial statements, Balanced Scorecards, operational reviews, reports, and presentations. What you are going to do next comes down to the forecasts, action plans, travel plans, new product development, cost and expectations.

This is all part of the communication process of who and what we are. It has a direct influence and reflects who we are and how well we perform. We need to ensure that we strive to continually and effectively communicate internally in a professional, meaningful, and structured manner, highlighting our progress and actions in support of the strategy. Remember, this communication is critical in the internal selling of ourselves and our organizations.

EXTERNAL COMMUNICATION

Advertise, sell, and again communicate. This is done through websites, conventions, direct mail, e-mail, telephone, texting, referrals, recommendations, social media, face to face selling, networking, and follow up. We need to continually communicate and state who we are, what we have to offer, why they should buy from us, what we've accomplished, our quality, the value of our product, what we can do for them, and how we can help them solve a problem.

We need to build trust, confidence, brand, brand loyalty, success, and curb appeal to go along with that concept. It's a package deal and we need to continuously sell the entire and all inclusive value package, our image.

In business, we have to sell ourselves and our organizations internally and externally and we need to do this all the time. If we go back to Patton, he was always talking about how "we are always advancing constantly" and we need to do the same thing in business. We need to be *Moving Forward* constantly. As a business and as leaders, like it or not, we are in a fishbowl and we are constantly being watched and judged. It is critical to always sell who and what you are, your brand. Be it. Sell it.

There is another quote that Patton used: "Attack, attack and attack some more." Change the word "attack" to "sell" and you have the same concept for business: "Sell, sell and sell some more."

Conclusion - Sales & Marketing

I learned very early in my career the value of taking care of the customer. If you take care of the customer, they will take care of you. Patton felt the same way. He knew that if he took care of his customers (his superiors and subordinates) that he would be in position to *Move Forward* with his career with more troops, responsibilities, and opportunities.

There is a quote that I use that came from the motivational speaker and sales guru, Zig Ziglar: "You can get everything in life you want, if you just help other people get what they want." I feel the same way. Patton did too. He knew that by getting his superiors what they wanted, that he could get what he wanted. Clear and simple.

While I was working in customer service and later in sales, by taking care of the customer, I was successful at bringing in additional work from current customers and new work from new customers. I took care of the customers and they took care of me.

I developed a strong, trusting relationship with many internal and external customers. By functioning under the "take care of the customer" adage, they knew that they could count on me to come through if they had a problem, large or small. I was there to help. I would always get the call to help others resolve a problem.

I am a firm believer that the Customer is #1. If you take care of him, everything else is easy. That's one of the reasons I've been successful with my business. I have developed that trust and rapport with my customers and those customers are now generating referrals because of that trust and performance. It's all part of the selling process.

By using a structured approach and specific and detailed action plans, I was able to win new work and develop new and strong customer relationships. Like Patton, I had a detailed and planned strategy and tactics to help get me where I wanted to go.

For instance, in the mid-1990s I worked for almost a year trying to get a contract with a new customer in Japan. They were heavily engaged with my competitor, but by developing and following my action plan and going to Japan every six weeks to meet with the decision makers, I was able to penetrate the organization, gain the trust and confidence of the key decision makers, and generate a signed contract for 100% of their work. That was over 15 years ago and from what I understand that contract and relationship are still in place. The process works.

I used this approach with another customer who was seriously considering pulling all their work and taking it to a competitor. This was an aftermarket business and the on-time delivery and door-to-door turnaround time on these components was terrible and the customer was rightly upset. We were not meeting his expectations. We had a better product, but we couldn't get it to the customer on time, effectively losing the whole trusting customer service aspect.

After my first visit with them, I developed an action plan specifically designed for this customer and this situation. Over the next year I was able to convince and internally sell within my own organization the remedy for the delivery issues. I also spent considerable time with the customer, working with their purchasing, engineering, production, and quality organizations, regaining their trust and confidence. I was there at least once a month working with them. And I'm not just talking about going in there and talking with them for an hour. I'm talking about a day and a half or two days at a time working the issues with them. To make a long story short, about a year later the customer sent out an RFQ for 100% of the business. It was winner-take-all event. We lost the contract on price, but because of the quality product, the high level of our customer service, and the trust and rapport I had gained with them, we kept all the business. Even though we came in second during the competition, we were able to get all the business not based on price, but on the value of the entire package.

While in sales, I learned the value of understanding my competition. I had files on each one of them and would keep them updated through my own recon exercises while dealing with customers, suppliers, trade shows, conferences, and anywhere else I could get the information. I was also able to gain great insight through use of the Internet. Some of my superiors were surprised and impressed at how much I knew about my competition. I would routinely get phone calls from people asking me, "Chuck, who is running such and such an organization? What are the annual sales for such and such? How many facilities do they have?" They knew that I had the information like Patton and his G2 section.

Like the military, I've always thought it critical to understand and know my opponent. Like Patton, I knew who they were, where they were, their strengths and weaknesses and in some cases, what they were up to.

I like to feel that I am a good communicator. What was not mentioned earlier was that Patton had great public speaking ability. He had a squeaky, high pitched voice, but he got his message across loud and clear. He was in his element on stage. Remember, he thought of himself as an actor playing a part on stage. He spoke the language of the audience. When he was speaking to the troops, it was loud and often profane because that was a language they understood. But as he started to talk up the chain of command his approach would change slightly, and it wasn't much different when he was talking to the general public. He played to his audience.

I too have a strong speaking ability. Some have said that I missed my calling and should have been a motivational speaker. Like Patton, I've been able to market myself and my organizations through strong communication up, down, and sideways on the organizational chart.

My operational review sessions and handouts were always several steps above those of my peers. They were clear, direct, professional, and to the point. My presentations have always been first rate. After some presentations I was invited to give them to the next higher level in the organization. I look at that as a tribute to myself and the quality of product that I was delivering. I feel that

I've been able to self promote to my benefit. Not as openly or directly as Patton, but well enough to get my points and accomplishments across. It has helped me *Move Forward* in my career. The way I'd put it is that I'm not as audacious as Patton, but I made my points and got the job done.

Since starting my own business, I feel that I've communicated and marketed it and myself very well. The website is up and running with regular updates. I've written and posted several case studies and articles. I have been focused on my own networking by attending several tradeshows and conferences. I belong to several professional organizations to assist with my marketing. I have a good web presence, both business and personal. If you were to Google my name I am up there quite a bit in a positive light. Like Patton, I have tried to manage my public image and presence. Only in today's environment, that is via the Internet.

I always strive to communicate, communicate, and communicate some more. That is one of the reasons for writing this book, to communicate about me and my business.

Sell, sell and sell some more.

A Battle Plan for Sales & Marketing

- Rule #1: Take Care of the Customer
  - o The customer is not the enemy
  - o Take care of the customer by providing a quality product, on time, with professional customer service and at a fair market value
  - o There are two types of customers: internal and external
- Primary Premise: Sales and marketing function to support operations and keep it fed with orders
- Once the vision and overall strategy are in place, sales then develops their own 3-5 objectives that support the overall business objectives and align with operations

- Once these objectives are established, sales then develops their own Sales Plan
  - o This plan includes market and competition analysis, target customers, products, specific action plans, travel plans, sales budget, trade shows, website, media
  - o Keep the plan simple and communicate it throughout the organization
  - o Once the plan is prepared, stay the course and follow through
  - o Track, measure, and report your progress
    - ▪ Prepare Actions Plans for areas that are underperforming
  - o Review the Sales Plan at least quarterly and adjust, adapt and overcome as necessary
- Use the Strategic Selling model to get beyond the traditional selling model
  - o Form strategic alliances with your key customers
  - o Get beyond the front line buyer and penetrate deeper
- Customers buy based on a need; Listen to them and tailor your approach as needed
- Understand your market
- Know everything you can about your competition
  - o Use the Internet; Google is your friend
  - o Don't be bashful; Ask
- Stick with your core competencies
- Salesman should not be rewarded on the sale alone
  - o Should also include elements of profitability and invoice collections
- Quoting:
  - o Do not let salesmen quote in a vacuum
    - ▪ They are part of the process, not the entire process
    - ▪ Get input and buy-in from all departments; It's a Team

- o Do not quote what is beyond your capability just to get the order
- o If you can't make money on the job, walk away
- Strive to openly and professionally communicate
  - o Internal and External
  - o Sell yourself; As the leader you are the #1 Salesman
  - o Manage your personal and professional image Network
  - o Use the media to your advantage

Chapter 8
Patton on Engineering and Quality

"Do your damnedest in an ostentatious manner."

"Make your plans fit the circumstances."

General George S. Patton

Patton was drawn to the saber very early in his childhood. If it weren't for his tank exploits, he might have been known for what he did with the saber before WWII. It was a fascination born in the stories told to him during his southern California childhood.

Patton was mesmerized by the stories of medieval times told by his father: The tales of Sir Lancelot, King Arthur, and the Knights of the Round Table. This actually played out in 1935 when he went to a costume party dressed as King Arthur and his wife Bea as Guinevere. When he was growing up, he had a horse named "Galahad," after King Arthur's horse.

There were also stories of his ancestors. His Confederate grandfather was killed during the Civil War while fighting and charging with his saber. As a youngster he played with his father's saber. Being from a relatively affluent family, he grew up with horses and swordsmanship became part of his life early on.

Like most young boys, he made many toy swords. There was one on which he inscribed "Lt. Gen. G.S. Patton." At the time, he didn't know what a Lieutenant General was nor the fate that the inscription carried. When he was older his father made him a sword and scabbard. Patton cherished it not only because of what it was, but also because it came from his father.

He became skilled at fencing and while in the Army, after careful study, felt a strong need to update the design of the saber and revamp its use in battle. At the time the sword was used primarily as a defensive weapon, more as a hacking tool. The tactic was similar to the way one beats carpets or rugs hanging over a clothesline.

Because of his fencing abilities and his horsemanship, after graduating from West Point, he was the Army's choice for the 1912 Stockholm Olympics.

There he would participate in the Pentathlon, which included fencing. He placed fifth overall.

After he finished the Olympics, he and his wife Bea spent some time in France and during that time, Patton took 10-14 days of private fencing lessons. His instructor was Adjutant Cle'ry in Saumur, France who was a renowned and European fencer. Patton intensely studied his fencing style and techniques.

After returning to the states, in 1913 he wrote an article for the *Army & Navy Journal* about the saber and it was well received. It gained him some exposure and notoriety, putting his name out in the market.

Then in June of 1913 he received orders to go to Saumur, France for the "purpose of perfecting yourself in swordsmanship." (His orders actually stated this.) He again would study under Cle'ry and he volunteered to pay for it at his own personal expense.

At the end of this training, he returned to Kansas and was appointed the first "Master of the Sword" at the Mounted Service School at Ft. Riley.

While at Ft. Riley, Patton developed the curriculum and taught the swordsmanship course using the techniques he learned from Cle'ry. The course, in true Patton fashion, was thorough, well thought out, and comprehensive. It was a whole new concept. Instead of the sword being used as a defensive hacking tool, it was now going to be used as an offense weapon involving more thrusting and charging.

Patton continued to "market" the need for a newly designed and updated Cavalry Saber. He was committed to it, he saw the need, and it was within his grasp. In 1913, Patton did design a new saber and it was adopted by the Army: The M-1913. The Army then ordered 20,000 units from the Springfield, MA Armory.

Patton was later sent to inspect and approve his new saber at the Springfield Armory. These events highlight and illustrate Patton's commitment not only to the improvement in the use and engineering of the saber, but also to its quality. He wanted to make sure it was being made correctly, to his standards and to his specifications. It was the last saber to be issued by the Army and it was carried until the Cavalry was absorbed into the Army Armor as part of the Army Reorganization Act of 1950.

He also wrote a small pocket sized manual titled "Saber Exercise" that was published in 1914 by the Chief of Staff Department of the Army. This manual showed how the new saber and tactics were to be used in battle.

As a side note, in the 1930s there was a movement afoot by the Cavalry Equipment Board to change the saber back to a defensive curved blade (Patton's was a straight blade) and they asked for Patton's opinion. He was not going to let it change and responded with a six page letter with his exact thoughts. The configuration did not change. It's not clear if this was because of Patton's input or the fact that the U.S. was on the brink of WWII.

Patton saw a need for an engineering improvement in the design and use of the saber, he committed himself to it, he was dedicated to it, he designed it, and he marketed (up through 1938) and sold it as well as refined the techniques for its use. The results were a significant amount of personal recognition and notoriety. For quite a while afterwards he was known as "Saber George." The saber was a very big part of his life. His efforts here highlight how he thought from both an engineering and process improvement perspective.

WORLD WAR I—TANKS

The tank was brand new in WWI. Patton saw that this was going to be the next big weapon system and technological advancement of the time. The technology was advanced and he could gain some notoriety with it and fulfill his vision, so he volunteered to lead the unit. He was the first army officer assigned to tanks in France.

As discussed earlier, while in France, Patton personally wrote the tank maintenance manuals and developed the tactics for its use and organized the U.S. Tank School.

Still committed to tanks, after the war he worked hard at writing and publishing his thoughts and comments related to revamping the tank and its tactics as well as hardware improvements, such as tank radio communication, armor, and weapons upgrades. Radio communication was new technology for the time and he pushed to get that integrated for enhanced communication between the tanks and the ground troops. He was committed to reengineering the tank to make it more efficient in battle and to ultimately save lives. He was so committed to tanks that during a high level demonstration he had his wife Bea drive one to illustrate the ease with which it could be handled. But post war America cut funding to the tank program and it was brought to a halt. He had a feeling the program was going to die so he transferred back into the Calvary to keep his career *Moving Forward*.

Again, Patton saw the tank as a major technological advancement that could save U.S. lives and, in his usual style, committed himself to making it better through improvements in design, tactics, and training.

TANKERS' UNIFORM, 1940

Because of his commitment to tanks, Patton realized that they weren't easiest to climb in and out of with their small, narrow hatches and that they were pretty dirty inside. So as an improvement, he designed a tanker's uniform. Patton felt the need for the tankers to stand out from the regular Army troops and in 1940 designed a new tankers uniform. It was a double breasted set of pea green coveralls, tailored at the waist, brass buttons running from the left waist up to the right shoulder and with a football helmet that had a gold ring halo around it. It gained Patton the nickname the "Green Hornet," which was a popular comic at the time and the uniform was never adopted. But none the less it does show Patton's attention to detail and his commitment to product development, improvement, and engineering. I give Patton three points for trying.

ENGINEERING AND QUALITY

"Wars may be fought with weapons, but they are won by men," Patton said. Battles may be won by the troops, but the quality and design (or engineering) of the weapons and tactics play large roles. In battle, if a piece of equipment breaks down or fails, soldiers die and the battle is lost. Whether it's tanks, ships, airplanes, weapons, equipment… everything must function as specified and designed in order to win in battle. This is a fundamental philosophy and approach for military equipment and systems.

I know that when I was in the Navy and launching off a carrier, I wanted everything in my aircraft functioning as it should. Things can get pretty exciting when you lose an engine or hydraulics while launching off the carrier.

The axiom of "he who has the better equipment, tactics, and training wins" is true not only in the military, but also in business.

The engineering and quality of military equipment must be first rate. This is a given. From my perspective, quality cannot be "inspected in." It's part of the strategy and culture and has to be "designed in" or "engineered in" as well as being "manufactured in." Quality is part of the process through concept, development, production, and use. Quality has to be built in from the very beginning and it has to work as designed (or better). It includes those performing the production or manufacturing work as well. Quality is a cultural mindset. Remember the old car commercial or motto "Quality is job one!" That's the type of thinking that needs to be incorporated into the engineering of new products. Engineering, quality, and production all work together to produce a product that meets or exceeds the customer's expectations. Again, this is just as true for business as it is for the military.

There is a Patton quote that comes to mind: "We have the finest food, the finest equipment, the best spirit, and the best men in the world. Why, by God, I actually pity those poor sons-of-bitches we're going up against. By God, I do." He was right! We did have the best of everything, and it was because we were committed and were "building in" and "designing in" high levels of quality during the engineering phase of the process.

Let's start by reiterating a key point. Engineering and quality are there to support operations and not the other way around. I have seen many organizations that, because of the strength of their engineering or quality departments, center on those departments versus operations. That's not the way it should be. The alignment is wrong. As discussed earlier, to be successful, the organization should focus on and center on operations. The entire organization is there to support operations so that an order can be fulfilled and shipped to a customer and the organization can make money (profit), and that is done through operations.

As mentioned earlier, in order for an organization to thrive and prosper, it first must take care of its customer. In order to take care of a customer, operations must deliver a product or service to the customer.

For engineering and quality that means they must strive to keep operations "fed." This means fed with drawings, specs, processes, policies, and procedures that will facilitate the manufacturing of a quality product, efficiently, at a specified cost (labor, material, processing, and testing) that will fulfill the needs and expectations of its customers. This engineering/quality mindset starts at the very beginning: It is part of the vision, strategy, and culture of the organization.

You have to get away from the mindset that "it's good enough." Let that go! We need to ask what does the customer want, can we fulfill his needs, and can we do it at a profit? The operative words here are "at a profit." It doesn't do any good to charge a dollar for something if it takes $1.50 to make it; you just can't do that for very long before you're out of business.

From a Patton perspective the question would be "Can we do what HQ is asking with the resources we have available and with minimal losses?" If we need to go from point A to point B with a specified type and number of vehicles and we have determined that it's going take 15,000 gallons of gasoline to get there and we only have access to 6,000 gallons in our fuel depot, we are not going to go very far and we won't be able to meet the customer's expectations if we only take 50% of the vehicles and still fall short of the destination.

There is a lot to be said about exceeding customer engineering and quality expectations. In many cases when a new product is being developed, in order to keep costs low, there is a tendency to build it to the bare minimum customer specifications or expectations.

We need to be making a profit by providing the customer with a product that meets his needs and expectations. Not by supplying him a product that falls short in meeting his specifications or by cutting corners and supplying inferior materials or processes. That does not meet his needs. We must meet his requirements or he will buy from someone else who will take care of those needs.

Patton said "Do more than is required of you." That mindset should be an integral part of our business development activities as well as the normal course of our daily performance. We need to continually strive to exceed customer expectations. That is what builds trust and that is the mindset and philosophy that wins orders.

I have seen many cases of a failure to fully understand the entire cost picture during the quoting process, when the business process does not allow for input from all other departments before a new product is quoted. As a result the quote is put together by the sales department in a vacuum with no input from operations, quality, or the supply chain. This is not conducive to successful product development or implementation. Once the quote is sent and the order is taken, the die has been cast. It's too late to make changes to affect the overall success or profitability of the program.

PRODUCT FAMILIES

In manufacturing there are four types of products:

"Runners" are the products we manufacture all the time and are basically routine. They flow as a normal part of our business and as such we fully understand costs, issues, flow, delivery, and quality. They are our part of our normal production flow and would be considered part of our core business.

Because the engineering is complete for the Runners and all the manufacturing issues have been resolved, we make these units very efficiently and our costs, quality, and delivery are predictable. The bottom line is that we make money on Runners because we've sorted out and addressed all the engineering issues. Everything done during the procurement, assembly, and test process works. They have no real issues or problems during the production process.

If a new order is taken for a Runner, the order acceptance process is relatively standard because all the information is accurate and readily available since we make these units all the time. However, before an order is accepted, operations should be (needs to be) consulted to ensure that there are not any resource, shop loading, or material issues as well and any specification issues or changes that may impact delivery or cost.

"Repeaters" are the products that we make every so often. We understand the flow, but because we don't manufacture them on a routine basis, our efficiencies, costs, and delivery can be somewhat unpredictable. We make them, but we are not as "good at" or efficient as we would be if they were Runners. Repeaters have a low to mid level of processing issues, which create mid-level frustration for cost and delivery. These are usually caused by engineering and operations documentation that may be somewhat vague, unclear, or not up to date because we don't want to take the time (Read: incur cost) since we don't make these products all the time. Because we're not as "good at" manufacturing Repeaters, our profit margins are lower than they are for Runners. From an engineering support aspect, it is critical to ensure that the engineering and production documentation be fully up to date so we can pretty much set the Repeater up as a Runner to ensure smooth operational effectiveness and cost control.

From a new order standpoint, the input from operations is crucial in ensuring that resources are available, and that costs, delivery, and quality are met. Quoting or taking orders for Repeaters without input from operations can make for unnecessary and painful surprises. Take the time and remedy the engineering issues on Repeaters. It will be well worth the effort from a cost and throughput perspective.

"Strangers" are products that we rarely manufacture and as such the operational challenges are higher than those seen for Runners or Repeaters. A perfect analogy is the changing of a bathroom faucet in our homes. It looks easy and in reality it is a fairly simple process. All that's required is turning off the water, loosening the nuts on the water lines, replacing the old faucet with the new one, and reversing the process. Sounds simple enough, right? About a 15 minute job? Not in my house. If I haven't done it recently, I can't find the "special" faucet wrench, the water lines end up leaking, and the sink plug mechanism doesn't work right. Long story short, I got it replaced, but it took two or three trips to the hardware store, cost about twice what I expected, and took four times longer than planned to complete. Now if I have to do another one the same day, well that one is fixed in record time because I now have the tools, the know-how and knowledge or the engineering mindset as to how to do it. Processing Strangers in manufacturing is the same type of experience. Once the order gets to the manufacturing floor we find that we've misplaced the tooling, don't fully understand the drawings or assembly instructions, and as a result the costs, timelines, and quality are not what they would be for a Runner. We routinely lose money when we manufacture Strangers. From my perspective, don't do them unless you are willing to remedy the issues beforehand. Walk away.

Sales folks have a tendency to quote and take customer orders for anything that has been made in the past. (Earlier we discussed the need for sales based on quotas or commissions). Don't do it! We are not good at it, we don't make any money at it, it gets in the way of the items we do make money on, and they are a nuisance.

In my organizations, we've strived to eliminate the Strangers for those reasons. We are not good at it, they get in the way, they're painful and costly to manufacture. In the end, no one is happy with the result.

If the strategy is to keep taking orders for Strangers, both engineering and operations need to ensure that the entire documentation package, tooling, and processes are complete, up to date, and efficient, so you don't have any manufacturing issues, and make money when it ships to the customer. If we don't make the commitment to take the time and do it right, then we need to walk away.

Have the courage (or audacity) to stick to your vision and strategy and "no quote" the Strangers if you're not committed to addressing the outdated or incomplete documentation, tooling, and processes. You and your organization will be better off for it. It's a tough decision, but one that needs to be made.

"New products" are exactly that, products which are brand new to the operation and organization and that are unknown and unproven. They can be "make or break" propositions. These are an entirely different animal and need to be handled differently. They are handled differently from the normal day-to-day engineering, operations, quality, and engineering perspective. It's a different mindset. For that reason, we will discuss New Product Introduction in greater detail.

NEW PRODUCT INTRODUCTION (NPI)

New Product Introduction or NPI is key to continued growth for any organization and if not done properly, can cause serious and potentially costly problems that adversely affect normal day-to-day production activities. When new products are introduced into production in a methodical and well thought out manner, however, it ends up being almost a seamless transition with minimal negative impact on the organization.

In most businesses, the typical NPI approach is to slip the development project into the normal day-to-day production work flow. They'll use the same resources, the same people, the same equipment, the same everything. They just drop the new development project in amongst the normal day-to-day work and wonder why it ends up in a big mess in both operations and engineering. This is because the engineering is incomplete or incorrect, specifications are not fully understood, the manufacturing process is not completely vetted, costs are not fully understood, and the tooling is not developed or proven out. The bottom line is transitioning a New Product into production without a complete, correct set of engineering drawings and comprehensive and proven assembly processes will result in a New Product Introduction (NPI) failure. Don't do it!

Mixing new development activities in with production does not work. The alignment and needs of each area are different and as a result you have conflict. The bottom line is that putting the two groups together holds back both areas and inhibits the organization's ability to *Go Forward*.

The approach that I have used successfully is to separate the development activities from the normal production activities or departments. Development and production are two different animals with different requirements and thought processes. They have two entirely different mindsets. And as a result, they do not mix well.

Production people think differently than people who develop new products. They speak different languages. Production people are structured, process and procedure oriented, and in most cases do not want to solve a problem. Development engineers are usually unstructured, free flowing thinkers who see no need to follow procedures.

Taking these two different mindsets and thought processes into consideration, do you see a conflict? Production and development departments are as related as cats and dogs.

What does work is dividing the organization into two separate, defined, self-contained, and dedicated areas of responsibility. The key words are dedicated resources. Two separate groups or entities. One is focused on normal production while the other is focused on development activities. They have two different charters or strategies and align their actions and accountabilities accordingly. In this way, you have placed the needed resources and emphasis on each area, thus eliminating conflict and allowing each area to function and support the overall strategy. Where it is impractical to dedicate a major piece of capital equipment to one area, this piece of equipment becomes a shared resource and to be scheduled accordingly. Everything else is dedicated to either the production or development cell with no overlap.

Let's break down a proper NPI into three distinct phases, where each area has its own mindset, skill set, and processes to make it function effectively.

- Prototype
- Pilot Line
- Production

"Prototypes" are thought up and put together by the dreamers within the organization. These prototypes are hand produced with minimal engineering documentation and function to prove out a concept. They are not made to ship to a customer as a conforming product. They are a "proof of concept" unit and not a conforming production unit.

Developmental dreamers are very intelligent engineers. They think outside the box and come up with some fantastic product ideas and concepts. They are always looking at developing new things and they are great at it! We need these types in our business if we want to continue to develop and grow with new products that will bring more business and more money.

Trying to put these folks in a structured environment is like herding cats. It doesn't work. They need to run somewhat free outside of the normal organizational policies and procedures.

They have great minds, but are not detail oriented, not standard in their approach, and not good at communicating or teaching. They have it in their head, so why can't you understand it? It's crystal clear to them and they can't comprehend why you don't understand. They speak a different language from that of the production folks and as such there is a language barrier. The dreamers come up with the concept of "yep, I see it." We can put this into here; that goes into there. In contrast the operations people just want to open up the box and take out the instructions and put it together. To take prototypes of this nature and drop them into production without the needed engineering documentation is disastrous, yet it happens every day.

Because it's new, the engineering is not understood or complete, the manufacturing process is not fully vetted, and they are not Runners, they do not get the correct amount of attention they need, suffer from lack of ownership, get in the way of normal production causing late deliveries of Runners, the costs are high, timelines slip, items are missed, quality is poor, frustration is high, delivery is late, and everyone including the customer is unhappy. It's a train wreck clear and simple.

Dropping a prototype directly into production is costly from not only an NPI perspective but also with the collateral damage it causes along the way. You are going to pay more by tossing it over the wall into operations than if you handed it off in a controlled and structured manner. "A pint of sweat will save a gallon of blood." It was true for Patton and it's just as true for the development of new products in business today. Take the time and do it right.

Patton said, "Haste and speed are not synonymous," and the same holds true with new product introduction. Throwing a prototype over the wall into production (in haste) without the complete and correct engineering documentation will result in excess cost, frustration, pain and suffering in both engineering and operations.

A phrase I like to use is "Why is there always enough time to do it over, but never enough time to do it right the first time?" Take the time to do it right and put the product into production in an efficient, structured, and logical manner. The amount of money, pain, and suffering will be worth it.

In the military development case, this is what would be a lab or testing environment or proving grounds for new weapons, equipment, or tactics. Think of the Lockheed Skunk Works. They did an outstanding job developing the U-2, SR-71 "Blackbird," F-117 "Nighthawk," F-22 "Raptor" and other very successful aircraft. They came up with the concept and prototypes that were later produced.

NEW PRODUCT INTRODUCTION FLOW

Now that the prototype is complete, to be effective at getting to a stable production process, the next step is the Pilot Line phase. This is the "bridge" or "transition phase" from prototype to production and is a very critical component that is too often overlooked (or overridden) as new products are rushed to production. It's not a prototype and it's not production. It's an intermediate transition phase.

This phase is handled by a team of process "tinkerers" who thrive on looking at a product or component and coming up with new and effective ways of making it better. They are not dreamers. They are what I call problem solving engineers with a skill set to think through a process from A to Z and figure out how to make it flow. They may be manufacturing engineers, industrial engineers, or just people who think differently. They are logical, systematic, and most of all, problem solvers. They are thinking all the time about how to make it work. These were the kids who would take apart dad's alarm clock just to see how it works. They think between the opposing mindsets of the "dreamers" and "production." These are the guys that link the two together.

The Pilot Line process is designed to "productionize" the overall process. Taking the hand-developed, hand-fit, proof of concept prototype and getting it ready for production while ensuring that what is manufactured meets the specifications in regards to form, fit, functionality, manufacturability, costs, serviceability, and durability of the entire end product. This includes establishing the bill of materials, the engineering drawings, design and proving out of the production tooling, assembly instructions, development and proving out of the production manufacturing processes, assembly, inspections, test instructions, and training. It provides everything needed to put the product into production effectively, efficiently, and painlessly as if it were a Runner.

The Pilot Line should also take into consideration the serviceability aspects of aftermarket or repair of the unit. They need to keep in mind how it can be repaired on the line, in the field, at a customer's location if needed, or as part of an MRO (Maintenance, Repair, and Overhaul). Ease of use and maintainability from a customer's perspective is an important engineering factor in keeping the customer satisfied. As an example, would you want to pull the engine out of your car to change the oil or spark plugs? Something similar happened with the Chevy Monza back in the 1970s. You actually had to jack up the engine in order to change one of the spark plugs just because that piece of the maintenance engineering wasn't built in. Maintainability and service of the product are critical to its acceptance and success.

In many cases this is done with a combination of engineering and production staff. It is a cross-functional team focused on one thing, putting that new product into production in an efficient, timely, and cost effective manner to ensure ease of manufacturability and costs at or below expectations.

A key aspect of the Pilot Line is that it is part of the NPI process with dedicated resources and as such is not done in conjunction with normal production. It operates and functions outside the normal day-to-day production activities and does not use production resources, thus eliminating production on the fly and conflicting priorities. This is a separate and dedicated cross-functional team with dedicated resources necessary to facilitate the Pilot Line process.

This may range from separate facilities, to dedicated equipment, dedicated manpower, different material storage and allocations and is not part of the normal inventory used for production purposes. It has different deliverables, costing, and even a separate organizational chart. With a separate supporting strategy, but one focused only on getting the new product into manufacturing effectively, efficiently, and painlessly.

The Pilot Line phase is also where the standardization of materials, processes, tooling, testing, and sub-components comes into play. I've seen many cases where two different engineers design a very similar product and use a completely different set of materials, sub components, special processes, or different tolerances to make almost the same product. This drives costs, inventory, and potential manufacturing issues because if it's not standard out on the floor, it leads to a great deal of confusion and associated cost issues.

The Pilot Line phase is key to attaining manufacturing and product standardization within the organization. This is where it all comes together. At this phase of the process these key and critical engineering and business decisions need to be made. Making changes after a component is put into production is too late. To change it then affects cost, configuration management, inventory, on time delivery, throughput, and efficiencies.

I've gone as far as telling the Pilot Line folks that they need to "Gumbert Proof" the process. (I used to say "idiot proof" but that upset the folks in HR.) What I mean by that is if I can read and follow the work instructions and understand the drawings, open the box of parts, and make a conforming product, they've accomplished their task. Some of them have actually used me as their guinea pig: "Hey, Gumbert did it! That means anyone can do it!"

As a side note, in Patton's era (and in today's military environment) most of the key components of any military vehicle of the same class/type/size were interchangeable. You could swap out the primary components such as the engine, wheels, brakes, fenders, lights, gauges, and many other components and put them on any other vehicle of the same class and size. They used standardized parts.

In fact, the main drive components of a WWII two and a half ton truck were the same as those for the amphibious DUKW that was used to move troops and equipment over water and onto land. It was all standardized. This standardization was all done as part of the Pilot Line process and was part of the strategy. The vehicle ideas were developed by the "dreamers" and were put into production by the engineering "tinkers" of the Pilot Line. The Pilot Line kept them standardized.

The "Production Phase" is the final result of the Pilot Line. The mindset and skill set of the production line is one of, "I take it out of the box, I read the instructions, and I put it together using these instructions and tools and I'm done." They are the customer and receiver of the end product coming out of the Pilot Line.

Once the new product makes it to the shop floor, the manufacturing process works, it's predictable and there are no problems doing it. It's easy, simple and clear and flows without a hitch. It's production, A Runner. It happens the same way every time with no input or intervention. It just flows. The Pilot Line took the time to ensure the engineering and manufacturing processes were complete and correct. It is not what I call "production on the fly."

TECHNOLOGY

Patton was a firm believer in technology. The tank in WWI was a major leap for its time and Patton wanted to be a part of it. The use of cars instead of horses in his pursuit of Pancho Villa was a new concept. The airplane was coming into its own, so Patton got his pilot's license and purchased a Stinson airplane to help guide troop movements from above. He was on the cutting edge of technology for his time and made the investment both personally and financially to take advantage of it. He was always looking for more effective methods in tactics and equipment; weapons and technology was a big part of those improvements.

His motivation was different than ours in business, but keeping up with technology is just as important today in business as it was for Patton. We need to keep up with technology where it makes sense and provides a tangible benefit. This is whether it's a new product design, new and more efficient manufacturing equipment, MRP system, new software. You name it.

Technology is exploding at a phenomenal rate. The computer you have in your home today has more capability than all the computers used to send a man to the moon in the late 1960s. And they were housed in several air conditioned rooms!

Most people know that a laptop they purchased today is outdated within 12 months. Look at cell phone technology: We have gone from seeing the 1960s Star Trek fictitious flip type communicators all the way to mobile phones with cameras and internet connections in a relatively short amount of time. With all the features on mobile phones today, we've exceeded that Star Trek prop.

From a civilian perspective Global Positioning Systems or GPS were unheard of 20 years ago. But today the technology includes handheld units that are in our cars and even on our cell phones.

And then there's the Internet. (I think Al Gore did a great job designing it!)

Technology is changing constantly and we need to stay on the cutting edge in order to keep up with not only our competition, but also our customers. They want and expect more in regards to product capability and reliability. The technology is there. We just need to stay plugged in and find ways to work it into our business processes and products, improving efficiencies and lowering cost.

Key opportunities for keeping up with technology include tradeshows, conventions, publications, and customers. Listening to customers can be a goldmine of ideas for technology and product enhancements.

For example, a customer likes the way product ABC works, but if it could do DEF or XYZ as well, he'd be able to incorporate it into QRX model and so on. By listening to our customers we are in position to fix his problems and fulfill his needs and requirements. Technology is part of that process.

QUALITY

Quality. A big word. It means different things to different people and, according to Wikipedia, has a perceptual, conditional, and somewhat subjective attribute. Quality depends on how you want to look at it.

Quality is the aspect of operations that ensures that the end product meets the customer's expectations in regards to the form, fit, function, and specifications of the customer's order. It is not just inspecting parts and determining if they are right or wrong. They work with operations within a Quality System with procedures to ensure that these aspects of the product meet the customer's expectations. In many cases today that system is ISO9000 where the standard defines the requirements. To put it simply, "Say what you do, do what you say and prove it." The quality system is the mortar that holds the organizational bricks together. It defines how we conduct our normal operational business and activities.

This is critical because this quality system keeps us on track and standardizes procedures for everything we do from how we take an order, right on through design, ordering materials, training, tool control, supplier conformity, assembly and test instruction, calibration requirements, packaging… everything. It's all part of a process and part of the plan.

The Quality Department is there to support operations. They should not function as traffic cops looking for every opportunity to write operations a ticket for something they did wrong. But at times it can feel that way. They are part of the support function for the manufacturing process and as such have an integral role to play. They too need to be included early in any development or quoting activities to ensure we can and do meet the customer specifications. They too are part of the team.

Quality is all about how we conduct our business. It's the mindset of the entire organization. I think part of the manufacturing process is comparing how we build quality into the product versus inspecting it into the product. For me, inspecting quality into a product doesn't work. You have to build it in as part of the overall process. It's a mindset, or a culture. I had a machinist tell me once that it was not his job to make sure the component he machined was correct; that was Quality's job. That is definitely the wrong approach. Everyone within the organization from the president right down to the receptionist and shipping clerk are all part of the quality process. We need to ensure that they are included as part of the vision, strategy, alignment, action and accountability process.

Another aspect of quality is integrity and in some cases today this concept is lost. In today's business environment we are all being pushed hard for results and that push can easily result in degrading quality. Sometimes it's subtle, like letting something pass that is just a little out of spec, but can extend all the way to allowing components to ship to a customer that flat out do not meet spec and are nonconforming just to "Make the Month." This is just flat wrong!

When I interview a senior operations or quality person, I'll do some role playing. The scenario is that it's the last day of the month and a big shipment for a customer needs to go out that day. We've been beat up by corporate for missing shipments in the past and we've told them this morning that everything is hunky-dory and that making the sales number will not be a problem. The month is in the bag. After lunch it is brought to this senior person's attention that the big shipment may have a defect somewhere, it's not readily apparent, it's going to take some time to research, and it may not meet the customer's spec. Meanwhile, everyone who can offer assistance is out of the office and unavailable so the decision to ship the potentially nonconforming product rests with that individual. To make a long story short, when they are pushed heavily as to whether or not they would make the shipment, over 50% said they would, especially if we needed the dollars to "Make the Month." Needless to say, they didn't get hired.

Why did they make the shipment of potentially nonconforming product? Because they were afraid of losing their jobs if they didn't ship it. They did not have the courage to stand behind their standards and convictions. Instead, they relaxed their integrity and looked the other way.

It was a problem of the company leadership, strategy, and culture, because it allowed the shipment. As business leaders we need to foster a culture where integrity is first and foremost.

In battle, if a nonconforming piece of equipment or ammunition fails, then people may be wounded or killed. The same holds true for many industries in the business world. Put a critical nonconforming component in an aircraft and it fails, and people could die as well if that airplane falls out of the sky.

As leaders you need to have the courage to stand by your convictions and maintain your integrity. My thoughts have always been that if there is a question as to whether or not a component conforms, then there is no question: It doesn't! Personally, I've missed shipments as a result and have felt the resulting corporate pain from above, but I sleep well at night.

"Be willing to make decisions. That's the most important quality in a good leader," and remember that "Moral courage is the most valuable and usually the most absent characteristic in men." Make the tough decisions and foster an environment of high integrity.

Conclusion - Engineering & Quality

Thus far, we've talked a lot about how important engineering and quality are to operations and the overall success of the business. Patton believed that. In fact he lived it.

During my career, I've done the same. I've always strived to *Go Forward* with engineering to improve the performance of the organization, its processes and products. It's not only from a financial perspective, but deeply rooted in the organizational strategy and was part of the overall business culture.

From an engineering and quality standpoint, I've always strived to build quality into a product. It wasn't easy, but through determination, leading, and coaching, I've been able to incorporate quality into the businesses I have led.

Patton's product was his troops and their capabilities and he did an outstanding job building quality into his product. For whatever reason, I have always had an innate ability to look at something like a business or operational process and see a better and more efficient way to do it. This has been true for shop floor operations, process flow, and product process improvements. Like Patton, I find myself always looking for improvements in how things are done. Like Patton, I'll formulate them and put them into practice.

In most cases they've worked and proven to be beneficial and have become part of the normal course of business. But in some cases they didn't work and, like Patton's Tankers uniform, were never adopted. But I live by the principles that "You're never beaten until you admit it" and "Take calculated risks."

Thinking and visualizing engineering process improvements have proven to be very helpful in my success leading operational turnarounds. It just comes naturally to me.

Patton had a knack for improving the organizations he led including II Corps in Northern Africa, the 7th Army in Sicily, and the 3rd Army in France. He helped them *Move Forward* and *Accelerate* their *Performance*. I have a knack for remedying underperforming processes and businesses and have helped them *Move Forward*.

Before the big push and drive for Lean Manufacturing, Six Sigma, and other process improvement initiatives, I was already out there making it happen. Think of the line from an old country and western song from the 1970s, "I was country when country wasn't cool." That was me. Patton, too, was not one to sit back and maintain the status quo. He was always *Going Forward* and looking for improvements.

This is true not only in business but also in my personal life, whether it's how items are stored and accessed in the files at home, organization in the garage, or the structured approach I take to a household project. It's all part of my makeup. It's me. At times it drives others crazy, but it's me.

I've led the efforts to make process improvement part of the culture. One organization very quickly reaped the benefits of a large customer order within a very short period of time as a result of incorporating these improvements.

Patton was a believer in getting things done through a structured and well thought out plan. He felt that the process and the discipline were key elements to success. I feel the same way. Put the plan together, follow it through, and have the courage to stay the course.

"You cannot be disciplined in great things and undisciplined in small things." This is just as true for having the discipline to get the engineering and quality complete and correct before transitioning a new product to production.

A Battle Plan for Engineering & Quality

- Primary Premise: Engineering and quality function to support operations
- Once the vision and overall strategy are in place, engineering and quality then develop their own 3-5 objectives that support the overall business objectives and align with operations
- Once these objectives are established, engineering and quality then develop their own departmental plans
  - Keep the plan simple and communicate it throughout the organization
  - Once the plan is prepared, stay the course and follow through
- Be committed to quality and process improvements
- There are four types of products
  - Runners: Products we do on a routine basis
    - Engineering and processing complete and fully vetted
    - A stable production process with few issues
    - Very predictable timing and costs
  - Repeaters: Products done from time to time
    - Engineering and processing data is fairly complete
    - Experience some production issues
    - Margins generally lower than Runners
    - Action: Address and remedy the engineering and processing issues
  - Strangers: Products that are produced only once in a while
    - Non-routine products
    - Engineering is weak with heavy reliance on "Tribal Knowledge"

- Costs and timelines are always higher than expected
- Action: If you are unwilling to address and remedy the engineering and processing issues, do not take orders for Strangers
  o New Products: *Warning*: Do not develop new products in conjunction with normal production activities
    - Take the time to transition them into production in a structured and controlled manner
    - Throwing them over the wall results in higher costs, longer development times, frustration, and late deliveries
  o New products should be handled in a three phase process
    - Prototype:
      - Proof of Concept
      - Developed by Engineering dreamers
      - Minimal documentation or process control
    - Pilot Line:
      - The bridge between Prototypes and Production
      - Cross functional team
      - Develop and prove out the complete drawing package, tooling, processing, and testing requirements
      - End customer is production
    - Production:
      - Engineering and processing as a Runner
- Technology: Stay up to date and use it in your development and process improvement plans

- Quality
  - o It cannot be inspected in; It must be engineered and built into a product
  - o Is a mindset and culture that involves the entire organization
  - o Are members of the operations support team and are not the police
  - o It includes a system of operating that ensures customer specifications are met regarding form, fit, and function
  - o Includes integrity; Have the courage to stand behind your convictions

CHAPTER 9
PATTON ON LOGISTICS

"My soldiers can eat their waist belts, but my tanks need gas!"

"Gentlemen, the officer who doesn't know his communications and supply as well as his tactics is totally useless."

General George S. Patton

Shortly after D-Day in 1944, Patton and his 3rd Army arrived at Normandy and broke out of the hedgerow country, leading a healthy advance across France toward Germany as part of Operation Cobra. By mid-August, their supply lines stretched 300 to 400 miles, putting a major strain on the system and the advance. It was critical to keep a fresh supply of ammunition, weapons, food, supplies, and gasoline advancing toward the front. At this point during the offensive the only usable Allied port was miles away at Cherbourg on the Normandy coast and the front was moving east at a rapid pace.

After D-Day as the Allies began to advance, it quickly became necessary to come up with a method to keep the advancing troops supplied (a logistics process improvement). The advancing operational troops needed to be "fed" or supported with ammunition, weapons, food, supplies, replacements and, most importantly, gasoline in order to do as Patton insisted: "*Keep Moving Forward.*"

Keeping these troops supplied was a massive effort as they were consuming supplies at a rate of approximately 21,000 tons a day. Prior to D-Day, in preparation for the invasion, the French railroad system was destroyed by the Allies, so it was unavailable. This created a strong need to come up with an alternative method of moving materials inland in support of the advance. This method was The Red Ball Express.

The Red Ball Express was a railroad term of the time meaning Railroad Express Freight. In late August 1944 the Red Ball Express was formed, running from late August until mid November 1944. They established a major supply depot at Chartes, France, about 250 miles from Cherbourg. There were two one-way routes established that operated 24/7: a northern route bringing supplies to Chartes and a southern route for trucks returning to Cherbourg to pick up more supplies. These routes were for the Red Ball Express use only—no civilian traffic.

By mid-September the Red Ball express had reached Versailles just west of Paris and split in two lines: the northern route heading north of Paris to support the 1st Army and a southern route south of Paris to support Patton's 3rd Army.

At its peak, the Red Ball Express operated with almost 6,000 trucks and trailers and was moving 12,500 tons of supplies daily. This was a monumental and successful logistics accomplishment.

As was the case with Patton's 3rd Army and its need for supplies and gasoline as it rolled across France, the same holds true for supporting a business operations department. Operations must be kept "fed" and supplied with the raw materials necessary to support the flow of production. Logistics are the folks that make this all happen.

From a logistics standpoint, in order for a business to *Move Forward*, the shop floor or production line needs to be "fed" with the needed raw materials, components, sub-components, tools, supplies, hardware and equipment; everything it needs in order to keep it moving.

Let's once again highlight the fundamental philosophy: Logistics and all other business departments are there to support operations. Not the other way around.

These are key and critical elements of the organizational structure and operations cannot perform or be successful without them. The logistics chain needs to be aligned with operations and its actions and metrics focused on supporting operations.

Logistics also needs to function under the same Quality System discussed earlier. They are part of the team and need to function under the same set of system policies, guidelines, procedures, and deliverables.

From the military perspective, logistics definition is a critical component of the strategy. Without the needed supplies and the transportation resources to keep those supplies flowing, eventually that army runs out of supplies, ends up defenseless, and loses the battle.

Patton was always stretching his logistics chain and came up with innovative methods to keep it flowing. This included capturing enemy supply dumps and modifying their equipment to fit his needs as he did with captured German sparkplugs for use in the Allied Sherman tanks.

In business, logistics ensures that operations has all the material in each area and support areas to keep it "fed" with the right material, in the right quantity, at the right cost, at the right place, and at the right time. Not an easy task. If operations does not have the right material, at the right time and in the right place, the production line stops, costs increase, and customer on-time delivery slips or production stops. This is right in line with an army losing a battle because it didn't have the right supplies when and where they were needed.

The logistics group needs to have its own strategy that supports the overall business strategy. These strategies need to be aligned. This is really a simple premise, but one that is sometimes lost as the organization focuses on other areas of the business. In many cases, the logistics function is overlooked as being just another support function, but they are just as important or critical as any other. They are a member of the team focused on winning the game.

PLANNING AND THE PRODUCTION SCHEDULE

As we talked about in the operations section, we need to keep the customer (internal and external) satisfied and the underlying premise here is that we ship a conforming product on time. To put it another way, "Schedule is King."

The production schedule is a key concept and tool of the business. It is the throughput roadmap and timeline for operations. It's the flow controlling document, which dictates and sets the priorities for the entire organization. It sets the stage for not only what is going to be done today, but also next week, next month, and many more months out. It sets the pace of the organization. And the supporting departments need to focus on keeping operations "fed" to support that schedule.

The schedule is indeed king and the overall controlling and priority setting document. It sets the pace for the entire organization as it sets the priorities and flow of the organizational needs and requirements. Business logistics includes not only the elements of getting the right material at the right place and at the right time, but also the underlying planning activities necessary to make it all come together. It includes all of the little things such as determining who will supply the material, the costs, when it needs to arrive, lead time, lot size ordering, shipping time and cost, tariffs or taxes, ITAR (International Traffic in Arms Regulations), etc. It's everything necessary to ensure that the right material gets to where it's supposed to be and that it arrives on time.

Ideally the planning and production schedule should come out of the MRP (Materials, Requirements Planning) system, but that system is only as good as the information loaded. Garbage in, garbage out. I've seen too many organizations running production schedules on pads of paper because the data in their MRP system is inaccurate or wrong.

You will also find it almost impossible to run a meaningful MRP system with constantly changing priorities and unknown issues regarding material flow, availability, and resource loading. These two functions, planning and the production schedule, are not easy tasks when the organization is not focused or committed to the strategy or philosophy of meeting customer on-time delivery.

Planning

Planning is part of the logistics function and a predictable production schedule is needed in order to drive the planning process. When involved in a turnaround or under-managed asset situations, I've seen many organizations where the production schedule is loose, undefined, fluid, and with daily (or hourly) changes due to a never-ending change in priorities from everywhere.

These include "lightning bolts" from upstairs to the program manager who brings in cookies to get her parts to the front of the line. They all have an adverse effect on a stable production schedule and the ability to make it meaningful and predictable.

This creates organizational chaos, shop floor confusion and frustration, slows down shop floor throughput, drives excess cost, unnecessary rework and unpredictable delivery schedules, and ultimately adversely affects productivity and on time delivery, thus creating an unsatisfied customer. We need to keep in mind that the goal is keeping the customer satisfied and a big part of that is on time delivery.

So then how are you able to effectively plan in these free floating environments? You can't. Everything is so chaotic that it's impossible to plan effectively beyond a one or two week window. So what happens? The organization resorts to operating "outside" the system on a series of manual spreadsheets that focus on the next two weeks of what they think they're going to need in order to make things happen.

This results is material "chasing" or "expediting" versus planning, a serious and costly process as parts are ordered on a expedited basis meaning more money, expedited freight costs, and more overtime as the organization tries to get parts where they are needed (or they think they are needed) as soon as they can. In this type of environment, rarely is the material where it should be, when it needs to be. Not only because the material may arrive later than thought, but also because the priorities may have changed and the material is no longer required. The entire organization functions in a reactionary, "fire-fighting" mode and chaos and increased costs invariably result.

Without the ability to effectively plan, you're only focused on the next short period of time (two to three weeks) and not the longer term. This is a recipe to maintain the chaos and continue to spend big money and fall well short of meeting customer expectations.

From there it degenerates into the "Make the Month" scenario we discussed earlier, again driving chaos and costs and degrades your on-time delivery. Until control of the production schedule is made stable, chaos will reign.

SCHEDULE

In looking at the overall process we need to plan effectively. To do that, you need an honest and stable production schedule. This is a fundamental premise.

It is critical to gain control of the schedule and make it predictable in order to plan effectively. Remember, "Schedule is King" and planning gets the right material to the right place at the right time and you can't get that without a production schedule. The production schedule is your plan.

The basis for an effective production schedule that is focused on meeting customer on time delivery is to work the oldest job first. No customer priorities. No money priorities. Only on-time delivery. It's prioritization of the production flow based on customer delivery dates and that breaks down to working things in that order and equates to working the oldest job first in each area. It's fundamental and it works.

This production schedule is practically "written in stone" and can't be changed without direct intervention by the senior operations representative. And that can't happen without a full understanding of the downstream and upstream ramifications.

For the businesses I've led, I've had success locking down the production schedule four to eight weeks out. Anything beyond that and there was too little visibility and too much "noise" in the system to effectively lock it down. Again: vision, strategy, alignment, action, and accountability. Do you see a pattern here?

LOGISTICS FLOW

Logistics brings this Patton quote to mind: "Success demands a high level of logistical and organizational competence."

Now look at the flow of a production order. You take the order, place purchase orders for the materials, receive the materials, place the materials into inventory, and when the time comes, you issue the materials to a shop floor

"Job," process the "Job" and send the end product to a customer. If the system works, this is all done on time, every time.

If we go back to the Logistics function to have the right parts at the right place at the right time, then we need to keep in mind that we need *all* of the right parts at the right place at the right time. Not just the majority of them. This includes materials from outside suppliers as well as from inside suppliers.

As an example, we can't build an automobile engine if we have everything except one of the pistons. That doesn't work. You need all of the pistons and all of the other parts in order to build the engine and complete the job. There is no way that a supplier on-time delivery of 75% will support a 100% customer delivery requirement with a normal production flow. It can't and won't happen.

Suppliers need to be held accountable for their own on-time delivery and the quality of their product just as our customers hold our organizations accountable. They too need to keep operations fed. This accountability is done through a series of options including Supplier Scorecards, audits to highlight production capacity, and recovery plans right down to ultimately moving the work to another supplier if the current supplier can't meet the deliveries and requirements set in the purchase order or contract.

The bottom line is that you can't finish a job on time if you don't start it on time and you can't start it on time with some of the materials missing. The only way that it can happen is if you add extra resources (Read: added cost) to expedite the job once the parts finally arrive.

This drives and feeds the production schedule chaos and will have a detrimental effect on quality. Remember: "Haste and speed are not synonymous."

An approach to help with this aspect that I've applied to logistics flow is to break the production process down into two functional areas.

Kitting: Get all the parts to the "kit" prior to starting the production process. This is the primary function of the logistics planning group. Like the customer delivery date, this kit date is firm and is a graded item on the Balanced

Scorecard. It is part of the operational flow and must be a major priority. The kit date and the need to meet it are elements of the strategy and must be a reinforced part of the organizational culture and mindset. Alignment, action, and accountability: The Three A's.

Production: The part of the organization that assembles the product, better known as operations, once the kit arrives.

In this way, you have a portion of the organization dedicated to getting all materials where they need to be: the kit before the job hits the production shop floor.

It also fits with the organizational alignment of keeping the operation *Moving Forward* by keeping it "fed" with the right parts and on time. If we go back to the BSC, we track customer on-time delivery, but we also need to track supplier on-time delivery and our own internal kit on-time delivery for operations. If these metrics are underperforming then, we will also need to understand the reason they're underperforming and prepare the supporting action plans.

COST OF MATERIALS

This is an amazing point of logistics and often overlooked. I have seen that many times the purchasing strategy is to buy strictly at the lowest price. This is a costly missed calculation and one that can be very painful to the organization if not managed properly. It's important to understand the full and comprehensive cost of purchasing materials.

If you get it cheaper, but the supplier is only 70% with on-time delivery, then what's the cost to the shop floor in regards to maintaining their own on-time delivery? From a Patton perspective, it won't support his battle plan if the ammunition, weapons, supplies, and air support are late 30% of the time and it won't support operations either.

If you get it cheaper, but it fails to meet your quality requirements 35% of the time, what's the cost to the shop floor as they try to maintain their on-time delivery, and the internal costs to handle the rework needed to make the component conform, or if necessary return it to a supplier?

From a Patton perspective, I'd hate to have only 65% of my ammunition fire when I'm in the middle of a battle. From my Navy flying days, I'd have a bad day if my F-14 tail hook failed 35% of the time while trying to land aboard the carrier. Operations needs conforming product as well if we expect it to function and maintain the production schedule.

In the case of tools, if you buy a cheaper product and it doesn't last as long, what's the long-term cost of replacing it more frequently? If you buy a larger piece of material because it's cheaper by the pound or in larger sizes, but operations needs to spend time and money cutting it to fit their requirements, what have you saved? What's the cost if you buy shelf-life limited material in bulk to save money, but then have to throw 50% of it away because you didn't use it before it expired?

There is a lot more to purchasing than buying at the lowest price. We need to fully understand the big picture and keep in mind our need to supply the right material to the right place at the right time and at the right total cost of acquisition.

Then there is the understanding of price negotiation. In many organizations, senior management assumes that their buyers are getting the best available pricing for the product they are buying. Often this is not the case. In today's businesses, we've cut costs to the bare minimum and that includes training. As a result, many buyers have received little training in negotiating with suppliers. In contrast, with our downturned economy, most organizations continue to send their sales teams to expensive sales training to learn how to maximize their selling price. This is like putting an untrained and inexperienced army recruit on the front line to fight highly trained German soldiers from the Eastern Front. Who do you think wins here?

Take the time and spend the money with purchasing departments, as well as everyone dealing with suppliers, to train and educate them in the beneficial and necessary negotiation skills needed in today's business environment.

STRATEGIC SUPPLIER ALLIANCES

Earlier we discussed establishing key alliances with our customers. As such we are supporting members of their team while supporting and contributing to their plans as one of their strategic suppliers. We need to be doing the same thing but in reverse with our supplier base. We need to forge alliances with our suppliers to help augment our plans and needs from both a developmental and on-going production basis. We need their insight and expertise. We need to make them partners in our business to help us solve our problems and issues.

We need these alliances to help us fulfill our strategy and have our business *Move Forward*.

CONCLUSION - LOGISTICS

In the organizations I've led, we've had a logistics strategy that supported the overall strategy, which included meeting the customer on-time delivery and quality requirements.

We strived to keep the operation fed with the right materials at the right place, at the right time, and at the right price. The logistics folks were an integral part of the team and were there to support operations.

We always had a production schedule (or battle plan) that highlighted what and when we were going to manufacture and the logistics folks were part of the team to make sure we got everything we required when we needed it. Like Patton, business operations cannot function without the comprehensive support of logistics.

My logistics purchasing and materials departments have been known to be resourceful in acquiring the materials needed to support operations. They used their initiative and worked trades, swaps, sold off unneeded or obsolete material and equipment, sold scrap, made special deals, and even used eBay to procure material needed to support the production schedule and keep the operation *Moving Forward*.

From the Patton perspective: "There are three ways men get what they want: By planning, by working and by praying. Any great military operation takes careful planning, or thinking. Then you must have well-trained troops to carry it out."

From the business perspective, this means that leading a successful business takes careful planning and feeding of the operations team to *Move Forward*.

A BATTLE PLAN FOR LOGISTICS

- Primary Premise: Logistics functions to support operations and keep it fed with raw material, components, sub-components, supplies, tools, hardware, equipment, and outside processing

- Once the vision and overall strategy are in place, logistics then develops their own 3-5 objectives that support the overall business objectives and align with operations

- Once these objectives are established, logistics then develops their own plan

  o This plan includes everything necessary to ensure that operations has the right parts, in the right quantity, at the right time and at the right price

  o Keep the plan simple and communicate it throughout the organization

  o Once the plan is prepared, stay the course and follow through

- The Production Schedule is King:

  o It must be stable and should be locked down for a finite period with limited changes

  o It sets the pace and establishes priorities for the entire organization

  o The production schedule is focused on customer on-time delivery and not sales value

  o Jobs are scheduled on an oldest job first basis

  o It should be system driven

- Planning and expediting are not synonymous
- Establish kit dates in advance of production assembly or processing dates
  - To deliver an order on time, you need to start on time
  - Must have all the parts on time
- Suppliers:
  - They too are part of the team and should be treated with respect
  - Must deliver conforming materials on time
  - Do not buy just based on price; See the bigger picture
  - Should be paid on time
  - Form strategic alliances with key suppliers
    - Have them function as a support function for the organization
- Provide your Logistics team effective negotiation training

CHAPTER 10
PATTON ON HUMAN RESOURCES

*"Wars are fought with weapons, but they are won by men.
It is the spirit of men who follow and of the men
who lead that gains victory."*

*"We cannot get anything across unless we talk the language
of the people we are trying to instruct."*

General George S. Patton

There were two sides to Patton. One was the hardened image of a natural warrior that he practiced and portrayed in public (although he disliked the "Blood and Guts" tag) and the other was a soft hearted man who was deeply religious, wrote poetry, and felt great sorrow when his troops were killed or wounded in battle.

Patton felt that if he had been a better leader and more competent as a soldier, then there wouldn't have been as many killed or wounded under his command. He often reflected on his capabilities and questioned himself. During the war, Patton was constantly visiting field hospitals where his wounded troops were recovering. He felt they were places of honor and there are many stories regarding these visits. He was deeply and emotionally moved by these experiences and felt a great sense of loss and self-doubt as a result. While making these visits, he would speak to the soldiers on a personal level, distribute meals, and award medals. He showed deep compassion for his troops. When his aid Captain Richard Jensen was killed in North Africa during the battle of El Guettar, Patton was moved by the loss to the point of tears and wrote a personal letter to his family, even including a lock of Captain Jensen's hair.

Patton was dedicated to his troops and had a great admiration for them. He cared about them and was proud of their accomplishments. He knew the importance of taking care of the welfare of his troops and he made sure they had everything— accommodations, food, clothing, supplies and anything else they needed.

Patton spent quite a bit of time visiting and mingling with his troops. He spoke to them on their level, including profanity, felt comfortable amongst them, and was always interested in his popularity. He wasn't interested in a popularity contest, but he wanted to know what they thought of him. He needed that feedback.

He would often drive up to the front with the sirens going and the oversized insignia posted just to make sure everyone took notice that he was there. He would drive to the front during the day and then fly back to the rear areas so no one would see him as retreating. He always portrayed the image of the caring leader to his troops because he did care about them. He was everywhere and could pop up at anytime. His troops knew that and most liked it!

Patton said that, "The more senior the officer, the more time he has to go to the front." He felt that officers needed to be seen in order to lead and understand the needs of their troops and he openly reprimanded those he felt did not meet that expectation.

Patton built and developed a strong staff and he had confidence in their skills, abilities, and experience (regardless of the feedback he got from his superiors) and would back them to the hilt.

But there was also a common expectation and understanding that you had to perform and that you would be held accountable for your performance. There was no doubt there. Patton expected results and you were expected to deliver.

From a communication standpoint Patton would receive short 20-minute briefings every day at 0800 and 1700 hours. These briefings were to get everyone aligned with the day's happenings and with what was important; Patton believed that you needed a "quick line of communication."

Patton knew the importance of training and was a firm believer in taking the time, money, and effort to do it. He said that "a pint of sweat will save a gallon of blood." He knew and believed that training would save lives. It was an important element of his strategy.

In August 1941, before the U.S. joined WWII, he planned and led a large 400,000 man mock-combat maneuver in Louisiana and eastern Texas to get his troops combat ready in the likelihood they would join the war. Later in 1941 he held similar training exercises in the Carolinas. In 1942 he developed the Desert Training Center (DTC) in California, Nevada, and Arizona for the purpose of getting troops ready for battle in North Africa. He approached these tasks with the same trademark drive and enthusiasm. He believed that training, training, and more training were necessary to prepare his troops for battle. You needed to train like you were going to fight.

Again, let's start with the premise that Human Resources (HR) is there to support operations and not the other way around. HR is an integral and critical part of the organizational team and their goals. HR objectives and actions need to be aligned with those of the organization and successful businesses cannot function properly without a competent and meaningful HR department.

However, I have seen organizations where HR is the controlling focal point of day-to-day activities. No changes can be made anywhere in the organization, right down to the color of the break room walls, without the approval of HR. They may be part of the team, but not necessarily the leader or coach of the team.

What is HR? In business it is HR's role and responsibility to ensure that the organization and the operations groups are supplied with the necessary and qualified human capital to meet the production schedule and ensure efficient cost operations. To me this includes the areas of recruitment, retention, training, compensation, accountability, ethics, and communication.

Without these items covered, the organization will not be in a position to foster growth and success. We must have qualified, trained, and competent human resources in order to *Move Forward* and *Accelerate Performance*.

In any organization it is important to have everyone understand where the organization is going and how we are going to get there—that's where the vision, strategy, alignment, actions, and accountability elements come into play. Once that's covered, it's necessary to get people focused and headed in the same direction.

How do we do that?

Many organizations do not have the right people in the right roles. As business leaders we need to take the time and assess our internal human capital skill sets to ensure we have the right folks in the right places. With turnarounds we need to make these assessments and the necessary people changes early in the process. This is critical if we are going to make the needed performance changes quickly.

These assessments can be made through a review of past performance reviews, observations, interviews, forced rankings, or input from HR. The key is to make the assessments early, get them on the bus and, more importantly, get them in the right seats on the bus. Sometimes, after the assessments you'll find that some don't belong on the bus at all. Have the courage to make the tough decision and remove them from the organization. You and the organization will be better off in the long run.

In many cases we have .22 caliber rounds in .44 caliber chambers or positions. These underpowered individuals fall short of performance expectations and end up holding back organizational performance. In many organizations we leave those .22 caliber employees in place because they're nice people or they have been here for 10 years and go out and hire another .22 caliber person to assist. Although it's a nice thing to do, it does not help the overall situation. You are paying two times the necessary salary to get a job done. This is not an efficient use of human capital or cost. Take the time and assess, upgrade or train the talent to fit the position requirements.

You can't win battles with mediocre strategy, tactics, and troops and it's the same in business. You'll need the strong "A" players on the team if you expect to execute the strategy, *Move Forward* and win. You can't win the Super Bowl if your team is populated with junior varsity talent. If necessary, upgrade your talent. It will pay large dividends down the road.

Once you have everyone in the right roles, you need to get them working together and heading in the same direction. That direction is set and fostered by having the right people and having their actions aligned to the vision and strategy of the business through the departmental strategies and individual goals.

TRAINING

As discussed earlier, Patton was a strong believer and advocate for training. Again his quote of "A pint of sweat will save a gallon blood" rings true. He trained, and trained and trained his troops until they got it right and could do it without thinking. Because of this, he reaped the results in battle.

While learning to fly high performance military aircraft, we did the same thing. We trained, trained, and trained some more until we could perform the maneuvers without thinking. When the time came to perform the maneuver, it came naturally. This is a key aspect when you're attempting to land aboard the carrier or involved in an in-flight emergency. Because of the training, the actions are automatic.

In many businesses today, training is something we do only to meet the minimal federal, state, local, or corporate requirements. We do it because we have to. Many businesses don't see the benefit or need for training. In our businesses, many have cut training budgets or dropped training altogether as they try to reduce costs and reinforce the bottom line. It's believed that it's inconvenient and gets in the way of what we really need to be doing or that we don't have the time for training. It detracts from our efficiencies on the floor and it costs money. During the budgeting process, training is often left out.

Or try the famous "I've been doing this for XX years and know what I'm doing" speech. Again, I'll go back to the vision and strategy discussion. An aspect that detracts from our commitment to training is the lack of tangible evidence that it works. In some cases the short term cost benefit analysis is not there.

I once worked with a company that spent big money on training folks about the elements of process improvement and they told me how they saved big money as a result of that training. Based on these stories, at face value it sounded like they had really made some serious inroads. But after looking at the financials, the positive results couldn't be seen. The labor and material margins hadn't changed, nor had sales, the number of people, or inventory. Nothing really changed. Why?

The reason for the lack of financial changes was two-fold. First, the changes in performance were calculated based on incorporating everything recommended during the project, but not everything was implemented. Second, the changes were not sustained, meaning that they were not fully accepted and put into practice as part of the normal day-to-day activities. They didn't stick because there was a lack of organizational and personal alignment with the incorporation of those changes and a lack of resulting ownership. There was no follow through; it was just an event, not a life alternating "Ah-ha" event. No accountability. No one really saw the benefit, so things never really changed. But the reports sure looked great!

So what's the key to training making a difference? It's the dedication, commitment, and follow-through to that training. Its supporting component is the execution of the organizational strategy. Its purpose and benefit are clear and as a result the training makes a difference. It is part of the big picture where the training is identified and structured, and the benefits readily and visibly feed the strategy. It builds on the strategic foundation. You can see it.

Training for the sake of training or to make a report look good is meaningless. Training where the benefits are clearly understood by the organization, department, and individual is key to having that training make a difference.

We also need to understand the aspects and follow through on that training. How many times have we sent folks to seminars or other training only to have them come back and never see the results? Why? Because we as leaders have not provided the necessary feedback loop or the structure where that training can be used or implemented. Its benefit is not understood and as a result, it goes nowhere.

Patton recognized the benefits of effective, structured, and formal training. He fostered an atmosphere where training was accepted and expected and he was rewarded with the results during his campaigns in North Africa, Sicily, and France. Had it not been for the training his troops received, he never would have gotten to Bastogne (Battle of the Bulge) as soon as he did.

As business leaders, we too must incorporate structured training programs into our organizations. We need to understand the benefits of training for supporting our business strategies and provide the time and money to make it happen. If we don't, nothing will change. If we do, then like Patton, we will reap the benefits.

EMPLOYEE WELFARE

Patton understood the need to take care of the welfare of his troops and we need to do the same in business. If we take care of our troops, our employees, they will take care of us. He had strong admiration and respect for his troops and we as business leaders need to do the same for our employees.

When I take a tour of a business, I'm sometimes amazed at the conditions. While going through the office spaces, the office furnishings are first class, the carpets plush, a nice coffee or office break area and sparkling restrooms.

Then when I visit the operations areas, I see poor lighting, cluttered and dirty work spaces, machines leaking fluid, broken equipment, employees eating lunch at their work stations, and filthy "third world" restrooms. That tells me a lot about what leadership thinks of its employees.

Taking care of the employees is fundamental and includes supplying them with clean, well-lit working accommodations. You would be surprised by what keeping the restrooms clean will do for morale, loyalty, and productivity. It doesn't take much, but if you show you care, it will go a long way to keeping your organization *Moving Forward.*

SAFETY

Another aspect of employee welfare is safety. Patton cared greatly for his men and he felt terrible when they were killed or wounded in battle. He did his best to see that they had the leadership, equipment, tools, and training to minimize the losses on the battlefield and to be safe.

In business we need to do the same. We need to ensure that our employees are safe and we do that by providing them with the tools, equipment, and training to keep themselves and others safe. We need to go the extra mile when it comes to safety. We need to foster an environment where safety is consciously reviewed and taken seriously. We need to support and help identify safety issues and concerns.

A few questions regarding safety:

- When was the last time your organization had a fire drill? If there was a fire at your location, would you and your employees know what to do and where to go? Or if the fire alarm did go off, would everyone just ignore it and keep working?

- Is safety part of your organizational strategy? What metrics do you use? Are they on the Balanced Scorecard?

- Do you ever see an unsafe condition at your facility and ignore it?

- Have you been to a safety meeting lately?

- Have you ever disapproved funds for a potential safety item because of its cost and not offered an alternative?

- Have you ever had an employee get injured on the job and not know about it for days?

- Can you tell someone what your OSHA recordable rate is?

Once your organization sees that you as the business leader are conscious of safety and committed to the safety of the organization, then the rest of the organization will see it as part of their responsibility and become committed to it as well.

It's all part of an employee welfare program and needs to be included as part of the organizational strategy.

Employee Communication

Keeping the organization "fed" with information or communications is another key aspect of employee welfare and is part of the HR role and strategy. How's the organization doing? What new programs are coming down the pike? Are we going to shut down between Christmas and New Year? Who's that new person in engineering? Did we win or lose that big order from the ABC Company? With the downturn in the economy, are there any layoffs coming? How come the break schedule changed from 9:15 a.m. to 9:30 a.m.?

These are all questions that come up in the normal course of running a business. How do you communicate this information to your employees?

As a leader, Patton was among his troops all the time. He had briefings with his staff twice daily and he was always giving talks to his troops or communicating with them in written messages. Everyone knew what was going on and where they were going. Patton even sent everyone in 3rd Army a Christmas message that included his famous Battle of the Bulge weather prayer.

As business leaders we need to be doing the same; We need to constantly communicate with our employees and HR is at the heart of that communication.

Is the Vision Statement posted where everyone can see it? Do you routinely talk to your employees about what it is and what it means? Do they understand the strategy and how they fit and contribute to it? Do they know where you are going and how you are going to get there?

Employees like to see and hear from the leaders of the organization. The communication goes both ways. I've told people that I learn more about what's going on in my organization by walking through the facility and talking to the employees, than when sitting in staff meetings! If you're out there and you make yourself available, you'll be amazed at what you'll learn. It worked for Patton, it works for me, and it will work for you.

Monthly All Employee Meetings are another forum of useful communication. Everyone is in the same place and hears the same message. Put the information in their language. Patton did it and it worked for him. Do the same, but without the profanity.

This is also a perfect opportunity to provide recognition to those that have done something exceptional or out of the ordinary. Patton would award medals during similar sessions. As he put it, "Give credit where credit is due," and All Employee Meetings are the perfect venue to do just that.

As a subset of the All Employee Meetings are monthly Birthday Meetings where smaller groups meet with the senior leader to get business updates and ask questions. These low-key meetings provide participants with a good forum to ask the questions they are afraid to ask otherwise. It also lets them see and get to know the real you.

Bulletin boards are another avenue of effective communication. Posting the BSC and associated action plans shows everyone what the organization is doing and what actions are being taken. The key is to keep the information fresh and flowing. Don't let it get stale.

How about those employee announcements? The new guy in engineering, the promotion in finance, the award in quality, the engagement in purchasing, the birth announcement in operations…not just the business related items, but everything that touches the organization and its employees.

How's the Suggestion Box activity? What about the Monthly Newsletter?

By providing constant and meaningful communication, employee morale will improve and be maintained at a high level as they know what's taking place within the organization and feel part of the team. Communication within your organization is a reflection of you as a leader.

ACCOUNTABILITY

This section is going to be difficult for some to understand as the approach will not fit with today's business norms. Accountability is fundamental if the organization is going to grow, *Go Forward*, and prosper. If we recall from the chapter covering the Three A's, accountability is the last building block and it is just below Success in the Six Elements of Business Success pyramid. It is the final piece of what's needed to take the organization to that next level of performance, yet many organizations shy away from it.

SIX ELEMENTS OF BUSINESS SUCCESS

Accountability has a negative connotation in today's business environment. We are often too afraid or apprehensive to hold our people accountable. If I do then they may run to HR or the boss, they may not like us, we may be viewed as not being politically correct, if I fire them they may sue, if I write them up for performance issues then they may file legal claims for harassment, there might be an investigation, I may get a bad review… The list goes on. As leaders we need to have the courage and discipline to hold people accountable and make the tough decisions if we are going to *Move Forward*!

In the case of Patton, if people were not held accountable, the system would break down and people would die needlessly. In business it's clear and simple: We cannot meet our vision or strategic objectives if we do not hold people accountable for their performance. It has to be done. People need to perform or the organization fails to *Move Forward*.

Patton was a proponent of putting the best people in the best spots where they could succeed. His quote, "Select leaders for accomplishments and not affection," fits very well into the business world. Make the new hire and internal employee move decisions based on performance and not affection or popularity. Have the courage to put the right person in the right position for the right reasons. It's about performance.

In my mind, employees do not perform well for three reasons:

1. We have not provided them with the tools or training to ensure they can perform. Here we need to assess the task we've asked them to perform and make sure we've provided the necessary tools and training to do the job. Once we've done that, it's relatively simple to hold the individual accountable for his or her performance. If performance continues to be an issue, the options are to provide additional training or investigate whether individual has the capability or capacity to perform the function.

2. They lack the overall capability or capacity to perform the function or task presented. Here we need to assess the capability and capacity of the individual we've asked to perform the task. In some cases, regardless of how much training we provide, the individual cannot perform. It's beyond his or her capability. It's a tough call and one that, unfortunately, many leaders are hesitant to make.

An example would be trying to have me function as a jeweler, dentist, or watchmaker. Regardless of the training provided, I do not have the patience or the delicate touch needed for such intricate work. Placing me in that environment would result in poor performance and failure. It is beyond my capabilities.

3. They just don't care or want to perform. This performance issue is simple to remedy—they either "get with the program" and perform or you terminate their employment through the normal organizational disciplinary process.

In regards to making the tough decisions, I think it's important to point out that HR is part of the process and not the entire process, judge, or jury. They have input into the decision, but in order for this to happen effectively, HR's strategy, goals, and objectives need to align with the overall organizational goals. In many cases that means not getting the right talent (external as well as internal) into the right places within the organization, but working the performance accountability aspects as well.

I've seen numerous occasions where HR believes and thinks everyone can be "saved" and as a result of this philosophy, terminating someone for performance is a long, drawn out, and monumental process. The truth of the matter is that not everyone can be "saved" regardless of the training, coaching, and mentoring. Remember, for an organization to succeed, employees must perform and be accountable for their performance. And in some cases there will come a time when that performance is just not there, and you will need to make the tough decision and let him or her go. Employees need to be held accountable for their performance and HR helps by establishing the guidelines for the performance, actions, and accountability.

I'd like to offer a word of caution. In our quest to enhance the performance of our organizations and our reluctance to make the tough employee performance decisions, we may have a tendency to accept mediocre performance and/or take on the task of doing the work ourselves, filling in for their shortfalls. *Don't do it*. Make the assessment, make the decisions, and have the courage to follow through. It's a difficult decision, but it's one that we need to make as leaders. You cannot "save" everyone and it's not your fault. Make the decision and move on.

PERFORMANCE REVIEWS

I'm amazed at some of the performance reviews I've read in employee files. After reading them you're ready to recommend them for sainthood, but after observing their performance and receiving feedback, it's clear that the performance reviews given do not accurately reflect actual performance. The manager (or the culture) did not have the courage to provide "Johnny" with an honest, truthful evaluation and feedback regarding his performance.

This is unfair to "Johnny" because he is unaware that he is not performing and it's unfair to everyone else because he is unknowingly holding back the performance of the entire organization. Then when it finally comes time to let "Johnny" go because of his performance, there is nothing in his file that reflects his real performance. In fact, he's a top performer!

As business leaders, we need to provide employees honest and realistic feedback regarding their performance. Not everyone is or can be an above average performer. Have the courage to tell the truth. By the same token, we need to take the time during performance reviews to understand where the employee wants to take his or her career and help them plot the roadmap as to how they can get there. It's part of the process to *Move Forward* for them and the organization.

GOALS AND OBJECTIVES

Earlier we discussed the importance of vision, strategy, alignment, action, and accountability. A subset of those items are the individual employee goals and objectives or actions.

Each employee should have a series of three to six graded SMART goals and objectives. These items should be aligned with those of the department and be within the confines of what the employee can influence and accomplish.

If handled correctly, these goals and objectives will assist with driving organizational alignment and individual accountability by providing the necessary action feedback during performance reviews. Did the employee meet, fall short of, or exceed his or her goals and objectives? It's black or white.

These goals and objectives will also assist in driving alignment and accountability if they are tied to a structured incentive compensation or bonus program where the employee's pay-out is directly tied to his or her performance. If he or she meets the objectives, then he or she receives a predetermined and communicated monetary pay out. It's a pay for performance plan.

This doubles as another method to provide employees with performance feedback: They get paid for it.

Accountability, as uncomfortable and controversial as it is, is a critical component in *Accelerating Performance* of an organization. As leaders we need to foster an environment where open and honest feedback is accepted and expected, where the rewards match the performance.

CONCLUSION - HUMAN RESOURCES

During my career I've always strived to care for the welfare of my employees. My troops. This was done as part of the overall plan. Like Patton, I've worked to keep everyone informed as to what was going on in the business. We did this through monthly All Employee Meetings, newsletters (in some cases we even mailed them home so the spouse could read it) and the posting of performance metrics and Action Plans.

There were the impromptu BBQs served by the staff, ice cream showing up on hot days, spot bonus pay-outs, letters of appreciation, Thank You cards for a job well done, facility upgrades and updates, etc. The larger aspect was spending as much time as possible out on the shop floor with the employees. It worked for Patton and it's worked for me.

I've been chastised as a senior leader for spending too much time in the shop. Patton was criticized for spending too much time at the front. I still stick my head in the employee restrooms to see if they are clean. I still feel it necessary to be out amongst the team to see firsthand what's happening on the floor and in the office spaces, to see and listen to the employees' thoughts, comments, and ideas.

Like Patton, I'm liable to pop up anywhere and at any time. That includes third shift and weekends. Not as an "I'm going to catch them doing something wrong," but as an active need to listen, to see if everything is okay and that they have everything they need.

I've functioned under the mantra that you can't help them if you don't know or understand the problem or issue. You have to be there.

Like Patton, I tried to keep my employees safe. Any time I see an unsafe condition, I try to rectify it immediately even if it means spending money to do it. I've dropped in on safety meetings. I've supported, fostered, and participated in mock injury and safety scenarios on the shop floor.

In the businesses I've run, I expect to be notified immediately any time an employee is injured. Like Patton, I feel terrible when someone gets hurt in my facility and look at it as a failure on my part when it happens. Yes, I too have a soft side.

I am also big on training, but training that is structured and set up as part of the overall plan. It's part of the vision and strategy. It's understood from the beginning what it is, why it is, when it is, how much it will cost, and how it will benefit or support the strategy and the organization.

Like Patton, I'm big on accountability and it has been a dynamic topic for me during my career. For the past 15 years, I've been handling financial and operational turnarounds and have had to make tough decisions. Think of Patton and his move to take over the underperforming II Corps in Northern Africa.

If the business is in trouble and rapidly getting worse, then you're up against the clock as time is running out. Gaining control of cash, the schedule, and setting the direction, operational priorities are a big and emotional part of that turnaround or *Moving Forward* transformation. In most cases the biggest issues have been with the performance and accountability of the staff and middle managers. In Patton's case, the officers.

As Patton understood, there is an element of discipline that is needed in these situations. Sometimes it's the little things like getting to work on time, getting to meetings on time and being prepared, getting reports or tasks completed on time. It starts there. Set the expectations and follow through. In other cases it's flat out noncompliance with the changes and directives. Those are easy to remedy.

Change is hard and it needs to be communicated and you need to lead it. Along the way, some won't feel the need to perform or be accountable and will be removed from the organization. Others will struggle through the changes, be trained and coached along the way, may have to be moved to areas where their capabilities and capacities are a better fit and as result became strong contributing members of the organization.

Like Patton I've felt that if an organization is going to *Move Forward* and *Accelerate Performance*, then as part of the strategy the organization needs to be held accountable to build and execute its plan, its communication, training, employee welfare, and accountability in order to be successful.

These are simple principles that are sometimes lost in today's business environment.

A Battle Plan for Human Resources

- Primary Premise: Human Resources functions to support operations and keep it fed with needed and qualified human capital

- Once the vision and overall strategy are in place, Human Resources then develops their own 3-5 objectives that support the overall business objectives and align with operations

- Once these objectives are established, Human Resources then develops their own plan

- o This plan includes everything necessary to ensure that operations has the needed human capital, training, communication, safety program, and employee procedures and policies in place

- o Keep the plan simple and communicate it throughout the organization

- o Once the plan is prepared, stay the course and follow through

- Get the right people in the right places and get them aligned

  - o Have the courage and discipline to make the tough decisions

- Take care of your employees

  - o This includes pay, benefits, training, safety, communication, facilities…

  - o As a leader, make yourself visible and available on the shop floor

- Treat employees with respect: It goes both ways

- Have faith and trust in your staff

- Communication:

  - o Human Resources is at the center of the communication plan

  - o Limit meetings and keep them short

  - o Employee communication includes, all employee meetings, bulletin boards, newsletters, postings, birthday meetings, letters of appreciation

- Accountability:

  - o For an organization to *Move Forward*, people must be held accountable for their performance

  - o People do not perform for three reasons and it's up to us as leaders to determine which one fits the situation:

    - ▪ They don't have the necessary tools or training

    - ▪ They do not have the necessary skill set, capability, or capacity

    - ▪ They just don't care

  - o Realize that you can't save everyone

o Set individual goals and objectives and establish the performance expectations

  ▪ Tie these goals and objectives to an incentive compensation plan

o Conduct structured and timely Performance Reviews

  ▪ Foster an environment that supports honest employee performance feedback

o When you have an underperforming staff member, do not take on the task yourself

- Play an active role in the Safety Program
- Training:
  o Key element in *Moving Forward*
  o Training should be structured as part of the overall plan and supports the strategy

CHAPTER 11
VICTORY IN ADVANCE

"There is one great thing that you men will be able to say after this war is over and you are home once again. You may be thankful that twenty years from now when you are sitting by the fireplace with your grandson on your knee and he asks you what you did in the great WWII, you won't have to cough, shift him to the other knee and say 'Well, your Granddaddy, shoveled shit in Louisiana.' No sir, you can look at him straight in the eye and say, 'Son, your Granddaddy rode with the Great Third Army and a son-of-a-bitch named Georgie Patton!'"

General George S. Patton
June 5th, 1944

I have heard it said that people look and act like their dogs and certain aspects of that comment ring true with General Patton and his white bull terrier named Willie.

Patton acquired his first bull terrier, Tank, in 1919 while stationed at Camp Meade, Maryland. He was taken with the breed and was impressed with its headstrong personality, strength, intelligence, determination, loyalty, playfulness, mischievousness, and fighting ability. Despite being deaf, Tank was one of the toughest dogs on the post. Like Patton with his dyslexia, Tank was able to overcome his shortfall.

In 1944 while stationed outside Knutsford, England and in command of the fictitious First U.S. Army Group (FUSAG), Patton felt the need for another bull terrier. He acquired Willie (originally named Punch) from a shelter in London. Punch had been owned by a pilot of the Royal Air Force who had been recently killed in action. Patton quickly renamed him William the Conqueror or Willie for short and he became Patton's constant companion. With his square jaw, dark eyes, muscular stance, commanding presence, and demeanor, Willie projected the tough warrior character projected by Patton as part of his image.

Willie was a constant part of daily life at Patton's HQ and there are many stories of Willie stealing letters and papers off Patton's desk, sitting in Patton's chair, being constantly underfoot, and just a general nuisance. Patton was a strong disciplinarian with his troops, but that didn't hold true for Willie. Willie received preferential treatment.

There is also a story of reporter and cartoonist Sgt. Bill Mauldin who was with the U.S. Army Stars and Stripes newspaper. In his cartoon Mauldin depicted the U.S. soldiers in what Patton thought was a less than favorable way. In 1945, Patton met with Mauldin in Luxemburg in an attempt to have

Mauldin clean up his characters' appearance in the cartoons. In Mauldin's book *The Brass Ring* he comments that when he entered the room that, "if ever a dog was suited to his master this one was. Willie had his beloved boss's expression and lacked only the ribbons and stars. I stood in that door staring into the four meanest eyes I'd ever seen." Willie emulated the image Patton projected.

Willie remained Patton's constant companion until Patton's death in December 1945. At that point, heartbroken over his master's death, Willie was sent back to the Patton's Green Meadows estate outside Boston where he lived out the rest of his life.

From his time at West Point (1904-1909), right up through the Allied defeat of the Germans in 1945, General Patton continually strived to fulfill his childhood vision of becoming a great military leader. In pursuit of that vision, while a cadet at West Point, Patton developed his own personal strategy as to how he was going to achieve that vision and from that early age, put his plan into action, stayed the course, and followed it through to a successful conclusion. Patton knew where he was going, aligned himself and others with his strategy, took the necessary actions, and held himself accountable along the way. It wasn't easy, but he ultimately attained his vision.

These same concepts proved successful for Patton in every one of his operations during his career. For each of his operations both before and during WWII, Patton had a specific and clear vision, a defined strategy to attain that vision, and the leadership to align the actions of his troops in the execution of that operational strategy, and he held everyone accountable along the way.

As a result of his accomplishments and reputation for getting the job done, Patton was given and took on the tough assignments. This is well illustrated in his successful turnaround of the II Corps in North Africa, his audacious push to Palermo and then onto Messina in Sicily in his efforts to prove the abilities of the U.S. soldier, his relentless 3rd Army drive across France after the D-Day invasion, and culminating in the operation to rescue the 101st Airborne in Bastogne during the Battle of the Bulge.

Today, General Patton is known as one of the great military leaders of WWII and history as a whole. The Allied results in North Africa, Sicily, Western Europe, and the outcome of WWII could have been much different had it not been for the leadership, vision and actions of General George S. Patton. George Patton did attain his childhood vision of becoming a great military leader.

The proven, simple and no nonsense principles that proved so successful for Patton are just as meaningful and hold true in our current business environment. With today's downturned economy, the success of a freewheeling business is not as easy as it might have been. It's not the same playing field as it was a few years ago and it's tougher to *Move Forward* or *Accelerate Performance* without a plan. In business today, it's more important than ever for leaders to establish and communicate their vision for the organization, to assist in the development of the strategy, and to lead the organization in the execution of that strategy, centered on operations while gaining the alignment, actions, and accountability along the way. Today, we cannot afford to be wandering generalities and need to keep our efforts focused if we are to be successful and fulfill our organizational vision. These basic concepts worked for Patton, and they are just as meaningful in today's business environment.

There are plenty of experts or consultants out in the marketplace with their magic formulas, complicated and politically correct approaches to helping businesses improve their performance. Some have strong points, but as mentioned earlier, many do not have the staying power of the simple concepts used by Patton. In order for change to make a difference in a business, it's important that it take hold and be sustainable. All through Patton's life he studied history and the traits and actions of successful historical leaders. He learned from those studies and was able to deploy what he learned into his strategies and actions. Patton's philosophy that we must "prepare for the unknown by studying how others in the past have coped with the unforeseeable and the unpredictable" underscores this point. As business leaders we need to do the same. We need to learn from the past so we do not waste time reinventing the wheel as we *Move Forward*.

We've discussed the aspects of leadership, the need for a vision and a strategy or plan to attain that vision, and the need to have our organizations aligned with their actions and accountability as we execute that strategy. These are not easy accomplishments in our downturned business economy. These efforts are compounded by the lack of leadership exhibited in some of our business and government organizations. As Patton once said, "we have many commanders and few leaders." Today more than ever, there is a need for strong leadership, someone to take a stand, set a course, and have the courage to stay that course as "You need to overcome the tug of people against you as you reach for high goals."

George S. Patton proved that through strong leadership, the establishment of a clear and well communicated vision, development of a defined strategy, and the ability to lead the organizational alignment, actions, and accountability, we can be successful in attaining our vision as we continually *Go Forward* and *Accelerate Performance*.

I'd like to finish with the closing monologue from the 1970 movie "Patton." Although it is not directly attributed to Patton, it is inspired by the legacy of the man, the visionary, the poet, and the leader.

"For over a thousand years, Roman conquerors returning from the wars enjoyed the honor of a triumph—a tumultuous parade. In the procession came trumpeters and musicians and strange animals from the conquered territories, together with carts laden with treasure and captured armaments. The conqueror rode in a triumphal chariot, the dazed prisoners walking in chains before him. Sometimes his children, robed in white, stood with him in the chariot, or rode the trace horses. A slave stood behind the conqueror, holding a golden crown, and whispering in his ear a warning: that all glory is fleeting."

APPENDIX
PATTON QUOTES

"A commander will command."

"A good plan, violently executed now, is better than a perfect plan next week."

"A good solution applied with vigor now is better than a perfect solution applied ten minutes later."

"A man of diffident manner will never inspire confidence. A cold reserve cannot beget enthusiasm."

"A piece of spaghetti or a military unit can only be led from the front end."

"Accept the challenges so that you can feel the exhilaration and victory."

"All very successful commanders are prima donnas and must be so treated."

"America loves a winner, and will not tolerate a loser, this is why America has never, and will never, lose a war."

"A pint of sweat will save a gallon of blood."

"As long as you attack them, they cannot find the time to attack you."

"Battle is an orgy of disorder."

"Be alert to the source of trouble."

"By perseverance, study, and eternal desire, any man can become great."

"Courage is fear holding on a minute longer."

"Discipline, which is but mutual trust and confidence, is the key to all success in peace or war."

"Do everything you ask of those you command."

"Do more than is required of you."

"Do not make excuses, whether it's your fault or not."

"Do your damnedest in an ostentatious manner all the time."

"Do your duty as you see it, and damn the consequences."

"Fame never yet found a man who waited to be found."

"Fixed fortifications are monuments to man's stupidity."

"Gentlemen, the officer who doesn't know his communications and supply as well as his tactics is totally useless."

"Genius is an immense capacity for taking pains."

"Give credit where it's due."

"Go Forward!!! Always Go Forward!!!"

"Good tactics can save even the worst strategy. Bad tactics will destroy even the best strategy."

"Haste and speed are not synonymous."

"I always believe in being prepared, even when I'm dressed in white tie and tails."

"I am a soldier, I fight where I am told, and I win where I fight."

"I don't measure a man's success by how high he climbs but how high he bounces when he hits bottom."

"I prefer a loyal staff officer to a brilliant one."

"I want you to know that I do not judge the efficiency of an officer by the calluses on his butt."

"If a man does his best, what else is there?"

"If everybody is thinking alike, then somebody isn't thinking."

"If I do my full duty, the rest will take care of itself."

"In case of doubt, attack."

"Inspiration does not come via coded messages, but by visible personality."

"It always made me mad to have to beg for opportunities to win battles."

"It is a horrid thought that one may be deprived of doing the only thing one is good at due to the exercise of 'free speech.'"

"It seems very queer that we invariably entrust the writing of our regulations for the next war to men totally devoid of anything but theoretical knowledge."

"It's the unconquerable soul of man, not the nature of the weapon he uses, that insures victory."

"Keep a quick line of communications."

"Lack of orders is no excuse for inaction."

"L'audace, l'audace, toujours l'audace."
("Audacity, Audacity, Always Audacity.")

"Lead me, follow me, or get out of my way."

"Live for something rather than die for nothing."

"Make your plans to fit the circumstances."

"Many soldiers are led to faulty ideas of war by knowing too much about too little."

"May God have mercy upon my enemies, because I won't."

"Moral courage is the most valuable and usually the most absent characteristic in men."

"My little dictionary does not have 'sycophant' in it, but every one of my divisions have."

"My soldiers can eat their waist belts, but my tanks need gas!"

"Never fight a battle when nothing is gained by winning."

"Never let the enemy pick the battle site."

"Never stop until you have gained the top or the grave."

"No good decision was ever made in a swivel chair."

"Nothing is ever done twice."

"Officers must assert themselves by example and by voice."

"One must choose a system and stick to it."

"Say what you mean and mean what you say."

"Select leaders for accomplishment and not affection."

"Strategy and tactics do not change; only the means of applying them is different."

"Success in war depends on the 'golden rules of war;' speed, simplicity, and boldness."

"Success is how you bounce on the bottom."

"Take calculated risks. That is quite different from being rash."

"The enemy is as ignorant of the situation as are we."

"The leader must be an actor."

"The more senior the officer, the more time he has to go to the front."

"The results prove that, as ever, leadership and audacity bring success."

"The soldier is the army."

"The soldier must know his objective and what he's doing at all times."

"There is a time to take counsel of your fears, and there is a time to never listen to any fear."

"There is only one type of discipline, perfect discipline."

"Untutored courage is useless in the face of educated bullets."

"War is not run on sentiment."

"War is simple, direct, and ruthless."

"Wars may be fought with weapons, but they are won by men."

"Watch what people are cynical about, and one can often discover what they lack."

"We can never get anything across unless we talk the language of the people we are trying to instruct."

"You are not beaten until you admit it."

"You don't have to hurry, you have to run like hell."

"You must be single-minded. Drive for the one thing on which you have decided."

"You need to overcome the tug of people against you as you reach for high goals."

"You shouldn't underestimate an enemy, but it is just as fatal to overestimate him."

"An Army is a team; lives, sleeps, eats, fights as a team. This individual heroic stuff is a lot of crap."

"A man must know his destiny. If he does not recognize it, then he is lost. By this I mean, once, twice, or at the very most, three times, fate will reach out and tap a man on the shoulder. If he has the imagination, he will turn around and fate will point out to him what fork in the road he should take, if he has the guts, he will take it."

"An incessant change of means to attain unalterable ends is always going on; we must take care not to let these sundry means undue eminence in the perspective of our minds; for, since the beginning, there has been an unending cycle of them, and for each its advocates have claimed adoption as the sole solution of successful war."

"Attack rapidly, ruthlessly, viciously, without rest, however tired and hungry you may be, the enemy will be more tire, more hungry. Keep punching."

"Battle is the most magnificent competition in which a human being can indulge. It brings out all that is best; it removes all that is base. All men are afraid in battle. The coward is the one who lets his fear overcome his sense of duty. Duty is the essence of manhood."

"If we take the generally accepted definition of bravery as a quality which knows no fear, I have never seen a brave man. All men are frightened. The more intelligent they are, the more they are frightened."

"I wish someone would listen to me. I have something which makes people reluctant to question me; perhaps I always have an answer based on truth and not based on 'bootlick.'"

"In landing operations, retreat is impossible, to surrender is as ignoble as it is foolish. Above all else remember that we as attackers have the initiative, we know exactly what we are going to do, while the enemy is ignorant of our intentions and can only parry our blows. We must retain this tremendous advantage by always attacking rapidly, ruthlessly, viciously, and without rest."

"In war the only sure defense is offense, and the efficiency of the offense depends on the warlike souls of those conducting it."

"It is foolish and wrong to mourn the men who died. Rather we should thank God that such men lived."

"Leadership is the thing that wins battles. I have it, but I'll be damned if I can define it. It probably consists of knowing what you want to do, and then doing it and getting mad as hell if anyone tries to get in your way. Self confidence and leadership are twin brothers."

"Many, who should know better, think that wars can be decided by soulless machines, rather than by the blood and anguish of brave men."

"Never stop being ambitious. You have but one life, live it to the fullest of glory and be willing to pay any price."

"Never tell people how to do things. Tell them what to do and they will surprise you with their ingenuity."

"No sane man is unafraid in battle, but discipline produces in him a form of vicarious courage."

"Nobody ever defended anything successfully. There is only attack, attack and attack some more."

"Personally, I am of the opinion that older men of experience, who have smelled powder and have been wounded, are of more value than mere youthful exuberance, which has not yet been disciplined. However, I seem to be in the minority in this belief."

"Prepare for the unknown by studying how others in the past have coped with the unforeseeable and the unpredictable."

"The great things a man does appear to be great only after they are done. When they are at hand, they are only normal decisions and are done without knowledge of their greatness."

"The leader must be an actor. He is unconvincing unless he lives the part. The fixed determination to acquire the 'Warrior Soul' and having acquired it, to conquer or perish with honor is the secret of victory."

"The most vital quality which a soldier can possess is self confidence; utter, complete, and bumptious. You can have doubts about your good looks, about your intelligence, or about your self control, but to win in war, you must have no doubt about your ability as a soldier."

"The obvious thing for the cavalryman to do is to accept the fighting machine as a partner, and prepare to meet more fully the demands of future warfare."

"The time to take counsel of your fears is before you make an important battle decision. That's the time to listen to every fear you can imagine! When you have collected all the facts and fears and made your decision, turn off all your fears and go ahead!"

"There has been a great deal of talk about loyalty from the bottom to the top. Loyalty from the top to the bottom is much more important, and also much less prevalent. It is this loyalty from the top to the bottom which binds juniors to their seniors with the strength of steel."

"This habit of commanding too far down, I believe, is inculcated at schools and maneuvers. Actually, a general should command one level down and know the positions of units two echelons down."

"Through the murk of fact and fable rises to our view this one truth; the history of war is the history of warriors; few in number but mighty in influence. Alexander, not Macedonia, conquered the world. Scipio, not Rome, destroyed Carthage. Marlborough, not the Allies, defeated France. Cromwell, not the Roundheads, dethroned Charles."

"War is the supreme test of man in which he rises to heights never approached in any other activity."

"Wars might be fought with weapons, but they are won by men. It is the spirit of the man who leads that gains the victory."

"We have many commanders and no leaders."

"When a surgeon decides in the course of an operation to change its objective, to splice that artery or cut deeper and remove another organ which he finds infected, he is not making a snap decision, but one based on years of knowledge, experience, and training. It is the same with professional soldiers."

Quotes were taken from the following sources:

http://www.generalpatton.com/quotes.html
© Estate of General George S. Patton Jr.
http://www.brainyquote.com/quotes/authors/g/george_s_patton.
html#ixzz1FDT98Egi

APA Style Citation
George S. Patton. (n.d.). BrainyQuote.com. Retrieved February 28, 2011, from BrainyQuote.com Web site: http://brainyquote.com/quotes/authors/g/george_s_patton_2.html

Chicago Style Citation
George S. Patton. BrainyQuote.com, Xplore Inc, 2011. http://brainyquote.com/quotes/authors/g/george_s_patton_2.html, accessed February 28, 2011.

MLA Style Citation
"George S. Patton." BrainyQuote.com. Xplore Inc, 2011. 28 February. 2011. http://brainyquote.com/quotes/authors/g/george_s_patton_2.html

Patton's Maxims from The George S. Patton, Jr. Historical Society

The Unknown Patton by Charles M. Province; MUR Publishers, 1996